10-P-0101

Appendix E

OIG Response to Comments on
OIG Scientific Analysis of Perchlorate
(External Review Draft)

On December 30, 2008, the OIG provided the environmental risk assessor community an opportunity to review and provide scientific comment on the *OIG Scientific Analysis of Perchlorate (External Review Draft)*. The OIG requested that scientific comments be submitted by March 10, 2009. The OIG received comments from the following seven federal and State offices:

- EPA Office of Water (OW)
- EPA Office of Research and Development (ORD)
- EPA Children's Health Protection and Environmental Education (OCHPEE)[1]
- U.S. Department of Defense (DOD) – Chemical Material Risk Management
- Comments from Dr. Pirkle, Dr. Osterloh, and Dr. Blount of the U.S. Department of Health & Human Services (DHHS) – Centers for Disease Control and Prevention (CDC)
- Alabama Department of Environmental Management
- Massachusetts Department of Environmental Protection (MassDEP)

The OIG also received comments from the following private and public organizations:

- Consultants in Epidemiology and Occupational Health, LLC
- Environmental Working Group (EWG)
- Human Health Risk Research, Inc.
- Intertox, Inc. (on behalf of the Perchlorate Study Group)
- Opdebeeck Consulting, Sàrl

If you have accessibility issues, contact our Office of Congressional, Public Affairs and Management at (202) 566-2391.

The OIG response to these comments is divided into two sections. The first section is our general response to issues raised. The second section contains specific responses to each submitter's individual comments. The OIG overall response to the comments follows:

---

[1] OCHPEE provided comments only on the previous internal discussion draft of the OIG Scientific Analysis of Perchlorate. OCHPEE did not comment on the external review draft version.

OIG General Overall Response to Comments

EPA has had varied opinions on the scientific merit of the *OIG Scientific Analysis of Perchlorate (External Review Draft)*. In January 2009, after consultation with EPA scientists, George Gray, the former ORD Assistant Administrator and EPA Science Advisor, recommended that the major finding of the *OIG Scientific Analysis of Perchlorate* should be reviewed by the National Academy of Sciences (NAS). By contrast, in March 2009, EPA's OW and ORD comments provided unfavorable opinions on the approach and findings presented in the *OIG Scientific Analysis of Perchlorate*. The opinions of the other commenters are both favorable and unfavorable. Although the scientific community has been actively studying perchlorate toxicity over the last 17 years – since EPA's issuance of a provisional RfD in 1992 – a consensus opinion on the toxicity of perchlorate eludes the risk assessor community.

Implementation of Cumulative Risk Assessments within EPA

Although a cumulative risk assessment represents a revolutionary advancement in the science of toxicology, ORD leadership has neither embraced the concept nor aggressively sought the development and validation of cumulative risk assessments. Since 1992, several NAS Committees and other scientific expert panels have instructed EPA to develop and implement cumulative risk assessments. However, over the last 18 years, ORD has not developed or implemented a cumulative risk assessment. Furthermore, ORD has not published Agency-wide guidance to implement cumulative risk assessments. ORD is still in the process of developing detailed, Agency-wide cumulative risk assessment guidance (EPA 2003, p 6). Furthermore, over the last 18 years, ORD has no demonstrated experience in proposing, conducting, or implementing a cumulative risk assessment on any class or group of chemicals. The closest ORD has come to considering a cumulative risk assessment was in 2007, when ORD tasked NAS to evaluate the potential of conducting a cumulative risk assessment for phthalates esters (NAS 2008a, p 141, appendix A).

By contrast, EPA's Office of Pesticide Programs (OPP) has successfully implemented cumulative risk assessments on several classes of pesticides that share the same mechanism of toxicity. Under the Food Quality Protection Act of 1996 (FQPA), Congress required EPA to conduct cumulative risk assessments on pesticides having a "common mechanism of toxicity." Within 6 years of the FQPA, OPP issued guidance to conduct cumulative risk assessments on pesticides sharing a common mechanism of toxicity (EPA 2002b). OPP issued its first cumulative risk assessment on organophosphates on June 10, 2002. To date, OPP has successfully completed four cumulative risk assessments on the following classes of pesticides: n-methyl carbamate, organophosphate, triazine, and chloroacetanilide. Therefore, OPP has successfully demonstrated that the science exists for EPA to perform cumulative risk assessments on chemicals sharing the same mechanism of toxicity.

Implementation of Quantitative, Mechanistic Dose-response Models in Risk Assessments

The use of a quantitative, mechanistic dose-response model has been identified and recommended to EPA to improve the scientific certainty and confidence in environmental risk assessments. Over the last 16 years, several expert committees have recommended the development of quantitative, mechanistic models to reduce the uncertainty in the risk characterization of chemical exposures to noncarcinogens. In 1994, NAS issued a report titled *Science and Judgment in Risk Assessment* that recommended that "EPA should develop biologically based quantitative methods for assessing the incidence and likelihood of noncancer effects in human populations resulting from chemical exposure. These methods should incorporate information on mechanisms of action and the differences in susceptibility among populations and individuals that could affect risk" (NAS 1994, p 10). In 2004, the Science Advisory Board (SAB) "strongly recommended the development of methodologies for quantitative uncertainty and variability analyses of toxicological parameters such as cancer unit risk values and reference doses" (EPA SAB 2006, p 16). In 2007, the NAS Toxicity Testing Committee recommended in its vision and strategy the development of a quantitative, mechanistic dose-response model of the cellular pathway that is perturbed by the environmental agent (NAS 2007). Therefore, based on these recommendations from experts in the field of risk assessment, the implementation of a quantitative, mechanistic dose-response model for exposure to noncarcinogens represents an improvement over the traditional risk assessment approach.

EPA Allows the Use of *In Vitro* Data to Conduct a Cumulative Risk Assessment

EPA ORD management rejects the use of *in vitro* data to establish relative potency factors for the four NIS stressors and their subsequent use in the OIG's cumulative risk assessment. ORD's comments assert that *in vitro* data do not take into account the biological complexities when *in vivo*. As such, ORD's comments identify that none of the four cumulative risk assessments performed in the pesticide program used *in vitro* data.

ORD's rejection of the use of *in vitro* data in risk assessments directly contradicts its opinion described in *EPA's Strategic Plan for Evaluating the Toxicity of Chemicals* (EPA 2009).[2] This ORD document is a blueprint for how EPA plans to pursue the direction and recommendations presented in the NAS report titled *Toxicity Testing in the Twenty-First Century: A Vision and A Strategy* (NAS 2007). This ORD document describes this vision as a "new scientific paradigm" for toxicity testing and risk assessment that decreases the reliance on traditional toxicity testing and risk assessment approaches (EPA 2009, p 3). This ORD document specifically identifies that this new scientific paradigm relies on using "data from subcellular or cell-based *in vitro* assays" to quantitatively characterize the perturbation of the biological process to conduct a "predictive risk assessment" (EPA 2009, p 8). Upon demonstrating the connection between the mechanism of action and the adverse outcome, this new scientific paradigm will "increase EPA's confidence that the Agency's [risk] assessments adequately protect human health" (EPA 2009, p 6). This document identifies that "an added benefit to the toxicity pathway approach is that mixtures or their components could be evaluated in this manner" (EPA 2009, p 9). Furthermore, this ORD document states that "realization and acceptance of this new approach will likely encounter numerous challenges" (EPA 2009, p 6) and "will likely be surrounded by some controversy" (EPA 2009, p 19). Furthermore, this ORD document identifies that the new science paradigm will require "institutional change" to gain "regulatory acceptance" and "will be an iterative process" that will likely take "more than a decade" (EPA 2009, p 7). Finally, this ORD document identifies that the use of *in vitro* data to develop a predictive risk assessment model "will come to replace much of the way toxicity

---

[2] Full reference citations contained in Appendix B

testing and risk assessments are conducted in the Agency today" (EPA 2009, p 19). Thus, the OIG's cumulative risk assessment is the first example of a predictive risk assessment model that implements ORD's new science paradigm. As identified in ORD's strategic plan, this progressive approach will be controversial. However, ORD's comments to the OIG rejecting the use of *in vitro* data in risk assessments clearly demonstrate that the ORD management is averse to implementing or even considering the merits of the new science paradigm.

ORD's categorical dismissal of the OIG's cumulative risk assessment because the relative potency factors for the sodium (Na^+)/iodide (I^-) symporter (NIS) stressors are based on *in vitro* data is inconsistent with its own guidance. ORD's *Strategic Plan for Evaluating the Toxicity of Chemicals* specifically identifies and allows using *in vitro* data to conduct predictive risk assessments. ORD's rationale that because *in vitro* data have not been used to date in an EPA cumulative risk assessment does not mean the approach is categorically disallowed. ORD's document identifies that the quantitative model of the perturbed biological step developed from the *in vitro* data has to "successfully and adequately predict human toxicological responses" (i.e., observed human adverse effects) (EPA 2009, p 16). Therefore, ORD's document allows the OIG approach of conducting a cumulative risk assessment if the predictions of the quantitative *in vitro* model are corroborated and verified with observed human adverse effects. Thus, ORD's comments should not center on whether a risk assessment can use *in vitro* data, but how well the quantitative *in vitro* model explains and predicts the observed human responses. If the quantitative model adequately explains and predicts the observed human responses, the quantitative *in vitro* model should be used to make risk-management decisions that protect public health. The OIG specifically provided corroboration and verification of the *in vitro* NIS Model for Competitive Inhibition with observed human adverse effects in Section 9.1.

ORD asserts that the limitations of *in vitro* data preclude it from being able to adequately predict the occurrence of adverse effects and nonadverse effects in humans. Although this is a stated opinion, ORD has not provided any data or information that disproves or discredits our cumulative risk characterization of this public health issue.

The Role of *In Vitro* Data in the OIG's Cumulative Risk Assessment

The use of the *in vitro* data is only part of the OIG's cumulative risk assessment. The OIG cumulative risk assessment recognizes that the total iodide uptake by the NIS is a function of both the amount of iodide available to the thyroid and the thyroid's total goitrogen load. An essential aspect of a risk assessment is to identify the exposure level that is associated with adverse effects in humans. In this instance, the exposure level is the NIS stress level that is associated with adverse effects in humans. Because the principal NIS stressor that limits the uptake of iodide by the thyroid is the lack of iodide in the diet, the OIG identified in the scientific literature the chronic exposure level to the lack of iodide under a typical total goitrogen load that is associated with adverse effects. This part of the OIG's cumulative risk assessment is the classic application of single chemical risk assessment approach to identify the NIS stress level under a typical total goitrogen load that is associated with adverse effects in humans. The lowest NIS stress level associated with adverse effect is referred to as the point of departure (POD). Therefore, the link between the lack of sufficient iodide in the diet and adverse effects in humans is made in our analysis without the use or application of the *in vitro* data that ORD objects to using. Thus, the OIG's finding that up to 6.9% of infants (i.e., 276,000 infants per year) are born with cognitive adverse effects because their mothers had insufficient iodide during pregnancy is not subject to the ORD's criticism of using *in vitro* data in a risk assessment.

The role of the *in vitro* data in OIG's cumulative risk assessment is to establish a working dose-response model that quantifies the amount of shift in the iodide uptake POD when the total goitrogen load acting on the thyroid is varied. Increasing the total goitrogen load increases the amount of NIS stress placed on the thyroid. Conversely, decreasing the total goitrogen load decreases the amount of NIS stress placed on the thyroid. The total goitrogen load is the combined NIS stressor acting on the thyroid from the concurrent exposure to the three NIS inhibitors (i.e., thiocyanate, nitrate, and perchlorate). EPA risk assessment guidance assumes the toxicity of individual chemicals in a chemical mixture add together (i.e., dose additivity) when the chemicals have the same "mode of action" and elicit the same effects. Since the three NIS inhibitors act through the same mechanism of toxicity, the individual exposures to each of the three NIS inhibitors must be combined to be compliant with EPA risk assessment guidance.

- Without relative potency information, the default condition in the EPA risk assessment guidance attributes the same relative toxicity to each NIS inhibitor (i.e., all three NIS inhibitors would have the relative potency value of 1). Because the measured blood serum concentrations of both thiocyanate and nitrate in humans are typically about 2800 times greater than the measured blood serum perchlorate, use of the default risk assessment condition for dose additivity would cause the amount of NIS inhibition contributed by perchlorate to be lower than that estimated in the OIG's cumulative risk assessment.

- Instead of using the default condition, the *in vitro* data in OIG's cumulative risk assessment allow the relative potency of the three NIS inhibitors to be assigned. The *in vitro* data identify that in-blood serum perchlorate is 15 times more potent as an inhibitor than thiocyanate and 240 times more potent as an inhibitor than nitrate. The relative potencies of the NIS inhibitors have been measured and independently corroborated multiple times over the last 50 years. The use of the *in vitro* data serves to increase the relative toxicity of perchlorate as compared to the other NIS inhibitors. However, this increased relative toxicity of perchlorate is not sufficient to represent more than about 0.31% of the body's total goitrogen load at a 95th percentile perchlorate exposure level found in the U.S. population. At the 95th percentile perchlorate exposure level found in the U.S. population, the perchlorate relative potency factor would have to be 100 times greater for the NIS inhibition contribution from perchlorate to increase the body's total goitrogen load by about 15%. This is still less than the annual variation observed in the body's total goitrogen load as the result of season variation in the composition of the diet. Therefore, the uncertainty in the relative potency factors for the three NIS inhibitors is not sufficiently large to change the findings of the OIG cumulative risk assessment.

Application of Traditional RfD Risk Assessment Approach to Perchlorate

The comments by the EPA OW demonstrate a clear preference for applying the traditional noncancer risk assessment approach to perchlorate. In 1954, Dr. Lehman and Dr. Fitzhugh of the Food and Drug Administration (FDA) originally developed the traditional noncancer risk assessment approach and implemented it by establishing the "acceptable daily intake" (ADI) for trace amounts of pesticides and additives in food (NAS 2001, p 25). The ADI is derived by dividing the highest no-observed-adverse-effect-level (NOAEL) by safety factors (Barnes 1998, p 474). If the NOAEL is from a human study, the original Lehman and Fitzhugh Model derives an ADI by applying a 10-fold safety factor to the NOAEL to allow for human variability (Dorne 2005, p 21). If the NOAEL is from an animal study, the original Lehman and Fitzhugh Model derives an ADI by applying a 100-fold safety factor to the NOAEL to allow for both interspecies differences and human variability (Dorne 2005, p 21).

In 1988, EPA formally adopted FDA's ADI approach for assessing risk from noncarcinogens (Barnes 1988). However, the use of the FDA's terms *acceptable daily intake* and *safety factors* implies the false notion of an exposure level that is absolutely safe (i.e., absence of risk). Therefore, EPA replaced FDA's terms *acceptable daily allowance* and *safety factors* with the terms *Reference Dose (RfD)* and *uncertainty factors (UFs)*, respectively. Furthermore, EPA increased the number and type of uncertainty factors that could be applied while deriving an RfD. Of critical importance is that EPA derives an RfD from an adverse effect. The original EPA guidance specifically identifies that an RfD is determined by applying UFs to a NOAEL (Barnes 1988, p 480; EPA 1993, section 1.3.2.3). Furthermore, EPA continues to define an RfD as being derived from an adverse effect (EPA 2002; IRIS 2007).

The principal adverse effect of concern from perchlorate exposure is the potential ability for perchlorate to cause hypothyroxinemia in the mother or fetus during pregnancy, resulting in an increased occurrence of permanent mental deficits in newborns. Hypothyroxinemia is a thyroid condition characterized by a decrease in the thyroxine (T_4) serum level and a normal or slightly elevated triiodothyronine (T_3) level, without an increase in thyroid- stimulating hormone (TSH) levels. The only exception to the use of an adverse effect to derive an RfD is that EPA risk assessment guidance allows the use of the immediate precursor to the adverse effect. Therefore, the immediate precursor to hypothyroxinemia is a statistically significant change in the T_4 thyroid hormone levels in the perchlorate-exposed group as compared to the control group. For clarification, the National Academy of Sciences (NAS) Committee to Assess the Health Implications of Perchlorate Ingestion (the NAS Committee) specifically identifies perchlorate's inhibition of iodide uptake by the thyroid as a nonadverse effect. In other words, the inhibition of iodide uptake is a no-observed-effect-level (NOEL). The NAS Committee states that the NOEL is the highest dose "at which there are no statistically or biological significant increases in the frequency or severity of any effect between the exposed population and its appropriate control" (NAS 2005, p 168). Therefore, the use of a NOEL to derive an RfD is inconsistent with EPA risk assessment guidance, and inconsistent with the RfD definition.

EPA's risk assessment criteria of deriving an RfD from an adverse effect is problematic in establishing an RfD for perchlorate. The NAS Committee states that adverse health effects have not been clearly demonstrated in any human population exposed to perchlorate (NAS 2005, p 177). Furthermore, although predicted by the Blount analysis (Blount 2006, table 6), multiple epidemiological studies have found no association between urinary perchlorate levels and free T_4 levels in the pregnant women with moderate to mild iodide deficiency. Therefore, EPA does not have a demonstrated adverse effect or its immediate precursor in humans from perchlorate exposure from which to derive an RfD in accordance with EPA risk assessment guidance. By contrast, adverse effects can be identified in humans exposed to excess NIS stressors using a cumulative risk assessment approach. Thus, our cumulative risk assessment derives a %TIU$_{(RfD)}$ (i.e., the RfD) from the observed adverse effects in humans which is in accordance with EPA risk assessment guidance.

On February 18, 2005, EPA established a perchlorate RfD derived from the nonadverse effect of iodide uptake inhibition (i.e., NOEL). EPA derived the perchlorate RfD from a non-adverse effect (i.e., NOEL) instead of an adverse effect (e.g., NOAEL); therefore, EPA has changed the environmental standard for protecting public health. A traditional risk assessment derives an RfD from an adverse effect in order to identify an exposure level that prevents the occurrence of the adverse effect in humans. By contrast, deriving a perchlorate RfD from the NOEL identifies an exposure level that prevents the occurrence of any detectable biological change in the body. The perchlorate RfD protects against all human biological effects from exposure which is a stricter public health criterion than limiting environmental exposure to protect against adverse effects in humans. This shift in risk management constitutes a significant change in environmental policy. Protecting against all biological effects is momentous change in the EPA's environmental standard for protecting public health – a change that has been made for perchlorate without any formal change in environmental policy, public law, environmental regulation, or EPA risk assessment guidance.

Uncertainty and Variability in the Traditional RfD Risk Assessment Approach

EPA comments express the preference for the continued use of the traditional RfD risk assessment approach to characterize the potential public health risk from perchlorate exposure. EPA ORD comments that the OIG's use of cumulative risk assessment is "premature" and may increase the "overall uncertainty" in the assessment. Therefore, an examination and comparison of the sources of uncertainty and variability between the tradition RfD risk assessment and the cumulative risk assessment of perchlorate will be considered.

EPA comments express confidence in the superiority of the traditional RfD risk assessment to better characterize the public health risk from perchlorate exposure. However, the traditional RfD risk assessment approach has a significant amount of uncertainty in the process and does not quantify the variability in the RfD value. In 1994, NAS issued a report titled *Science and Judgment in Risk Assessment,* which specifically identified that regulated industries, environmental organizations, and academicians have leveled a broad array of criticisms of EPA's traditional risk assessment processes (NAS 1994). These concerns specifically included "the lack of scientific data quantitatively relating chemical exposure to health risks" (NAS 1994, pp 5-6). Furthermore, this 1994 NAS report states that "EPA should develop biologically based quantitative methods for assessing the incidence and likelihood of non-cancer effects in human populations resulting from chemical exposure. These methods should incorporate information on mechanisms of action and differences in susceptibility among populations and individuals that could affect risk" (NAS 1994, p 10). Therefore, for at least 16 years, EPA has known of the weaknesses in the traditional risk assessment approach and the need to develop mechanistic, quantitative models defining the relationship between exposure and adverse effects to reduce the uncertainty in the risk assessment.

The following discusses the principal sources of scientific uncertainty and variability occurring during the establishment of the EPA perchlorate RfD. (Note: Sources are not intended to be exhaustive. Furthermore, some sources of uncertainty and variability overlap, but are discussed to illustrate a specific aspect of the issue):

- <u>Uncertainty in the Biological Response to a Low Uptake of Iodide</u> – The NAS Committee's mode-of-action model for perchlorate toxicity in humans identifies that the inadequate uptake of iodide by the thyroid results in hypothyroidism and would be the first adverse effect in humans (NAS 2005, p 166). However, the low uptake of iodide by the thyroid caused by iodide deficiency, which acts through the same mechanism of toxicity as perchlorate, induces hypothyroxinemia, not hypothyroidism (Obregon 2005). By contrast, overt hypothyroidism only occurs when the NIS stress of iodide deficiency is accompanied by the additional NIS stress of a high goitrogen load and/or selenium deficiency (Obregon 2005). Therefore, incorrectly identifying hypothyroidism as the first adverse effects in an adult weakens the confidence in EPA's risk characterization of perchlorate.

- <u>Uncertainty in Detecting Adverse Effects in Adults</u> – The NAS Committee states that adverse health effects have not been clearly demonstrated in any human population exposed to perchlorate (NAS, 2005, p 177). Furthermore, the NAS Committee specifically identifies perchlorate's inhibition of iodide uptake by the thyroid as a non-adverse effect (i.e., a no-observed-effect-level (NOEL)). Since an RfD is derived from an adverse effect, the inability to detect an adverse effect from perchlorate exposure (e.g., a NOAEL or lowest-observed-adverse-effect-level (LOAEL)) in any human population contributes a significant amount of uncertainty to the establishment of a perchlorate RfD.

- <u>Uncertainty in Identifying Adverse Effects in Children</u> – The NAS Committee suggested that for the "most sensitive population" (i.e., the fetus) (NAS 2005, p 27), the possible induction of hypothyroidism during pregnancy could possibly result in abnormal growth and development of the fetuses and children (NAS 2005, p 13). Furthermore, the NAS Committee states that the "epidemiologic evidence is inadequate to determine whether or not there is a causal association between perchlorate exposure and adverse neurodevelopmental outcomes in children" (NAS 2005, p 9). Furthermore, the NAS Committee identifies that there are "no adequate studies of maternal perchlorate exposure and neurodevelopmental outcomes in infants" (NAS 2005, p 10). Therefore, the specific types of cognitive deficit(s) expected to be observed in children from excessive maternal exposure have not been detected or identified. Without this information, EPA has not identified the public health risk to the cognitive development of children. If the public risk to cognitive development in children cannot be identified, EPA has difficulty justifying an environmental regulation to protect against a hazard that has not been identified or demonstrated. Thus, EPA's inability to identify a specific cognitive deficit in children from excessive maternal perchlorate exposure introduces considerable uncertainty into the risk characterization of perchlorate.

- Uncertainty in Dose-response for Most Sensitive Population – The dose-response curve is a fundamental element in characterizing the toxicity of a chemical. However, since adverse effects have not been observed in populations of adults, pregnant women, fetuses, nursing infants, or children, a dose response has not been established between the perchlorate exposure and the frequency or severity of adverse effects in any human population. Therefore, the lack of a perchlorate dose-response curve for adverse effects introduces considerable uncertainty into risk characterization of perchlorate.

  Point of clarification: The NAS Committee specifically emphasizes that the inhibition of iodide uptake is a nonadverse effect (NAS 2005, p 166). Therefore, the dose-response curve observed in the Greer study is the relationship between perchlorate exposure and a non-adverse effect. Therefore, the Greer data do not provide the dose-response relationship needed to characterize the occurrence of adverse effects from perchlorate exposure.

- Variability in Measuring Exposure – External dose is a poor measure of the actual internal exposure. The Clewell Perchlorate Physiologically-based Pharmacokinetic (PBPK) Model identifies the same external dose results in different levels of actual internal exposure (Clewell 2007). For example, the Clewell PBPK Model estimates that the same external perchlorate dose of 0.001 mg/kg-day results in elevated internal blood serum concentration in pregnant women, lactating women, neonates, and fetuses of 2.5 times, 4 times, 4 times, and 5 times the internal blood serum concentration found in an adult, respectively (Clewell 2007, p 423, table 4). This known difference in internal exposure across these subpopulations is not incorporated in a traditional RfD risk assessment.

- Uncertainty in Measuring the POD in the Sensitive Populations – In the Greer study, the POD was identified in adult males and females. However, the most sensitive population is the developing fetuses during pregnancy (NAS 2005, p 27). Therefore, the POD used was not determined in the most sensitive population, which introduces scientific uncertainty into the traditional risk assessment.

- Uncertainty in the Perchlorate RfD as a Function of Dietary Iodide Intake – The NAS Committee was charged to "consider the influence of iodide in the diet on the [perchlorate exposure] levels at which adverse effects would be observed" (NAS 2005, p 30). However, this charge is inconsistent with the traditional risk assessment approach that assumes away confounding variables. This practice avoids the difficulty of having to specifically quantify the confounding variable's effect on the occurrence or severity of an adverse effect. In the perchlorate risk assessment, neither the NAS Committee nor EPA attempted to quantify the effect that dietary iodide intake has on the perchlorate RfD. The practice of not incorporating confounding variables in traditional risk assessments is the impetus for the OW comment that dietary iodide intake should be treated as a "constant" in the traditional risk assessment approach.

By assuming the dietary iodide intake in the U.S. population is a constant, EPA has incorporated an unrealistic assumption into the risk assessment. CDC's National Health and Nutrition Examination Survey (NHANES) III identifies that urinary iodine levels in the 5th and 95th percentiles in the United States population are 30 ug/L and 525 ug/L, respectively (NAP 2000, table G-6). This survey identifies that the dietary iodide intake in the U.S. population varies by a factor of at least 17.5 times. Therefore, EPA's assumption that dietary iodide intake is a constant in the U.S. population introduces considerable uncertainty into the EPA's traditional RfD risk assessment of perchlorate.

Dietary iodide intake is an important biological factor that contributes to the thyroid's ability to uptake a sufficient amount of iodide to avoid adverse effects. The need to incorporate dietary iodide intake in the perchlorate risk assessment is expressed by the NAS Committee statement that the primary source of uncertainty "arises from the absence of data on possible effects from perchlorate" in pregnant women, their fetuses, and newborns with iodide deficiency (NAS 2005, p 18). The importance of dietary iodide intake is found in clinical observations in populations with endemic cretinism that identify iodide deficiency decreases the thyroid's tolerance for NIS inhibition. In other words, a decreased dietary iodide intake lowers the body's ability to tolerate NIS inhibition. Conversely, an increased dietary iodide intake raises the body's ability to tolerate NIS inhibition. However, neither the NAS Committee nor EPA attempt to quantify the effect that dietary iodide intake has on the body's ability to tolerate NIS inhibition. Therefore, dietary iodide intake introduces the primary source of scientific uncertainty into the establishment of the perchlorate RfD value.

- Variability in Perchlorate RfD as a Function of the Body's Goitrogen Load – EPA risk assessment guidance instructs risk assessors to aggregate the risk from chemicals sharing the same "mode of action" and elicit the same effect (EPA 1986; EPA 2000). Thiocyanate, nitrate, and perchlorate (i.e., NIS inhibitors) share the same mechanism of toxicity by inhibiting iodide uptake by the thyroid. The combined action of all three NIS inhibitors determines the total amount of inhibition acting on the thyroid (i.e., goitrogen load). Because the body is continuously exposed to all three NIS inhibitors, the body's goitrogen load is never zero. Therefore, the potential toxicity from perchlorate exposure needs to be evaluated in context with the body's typical goitrogen load.

A traditional RfD risk assessment considers the toxicity induced by a single chemical at a time. As such, the traditional RfD risk assessment for perchlorate assumes that the concurrent exposure to thiocyanate and nitrate are constant. However, this is a poor assumption because human exposure to thiocyanate and nitrate varies by more than a magnitude each. Furthermore, at typical NIS inhibitor exposure levels, perchlorate contributes only a small fraction of the body's total goitrogen load. Therefore, perchlorate exposure alone is a poor indicator of the body's total goitrogen load. Because the body's total goitrogen load is a major determinant of the NIS stress level acting on the thyroid, the amount of risk from perchlorate varies depending on the body's total goitrogen load. In practical terms, if the body's goitrogen load is high, the thyroid can tolerate less additional NIS inhibition from perchlorate without inducing adverse effects. Conversely, if the body's goitrogen load is low, the thyroid can tolerate more NIS inhibition from perchlorate without inducing adverse effects. Thus, the risk from perchlorate exposure is not constant and varies depending on the body's total goitrogen load. This variability introduces uncertainty into the establishment of the perchlorate RfD.

- Uncertainty in Incorporating Homeostasis – The nonadverse effect of inhibition of iodide uptake by the thyroid in humans was used to derive the perchlorate RfD. The Greer study measured the thyroid's short-term response to NIS inhibition. The Greer study did not evaluate the thyroid's biological ability to adapt to changes in NIS inhibition levels or the developing brain's biological ability to adapt to a decreased supply of T_4 hormone through the activation of the brain's D2-D3 deiodinase compensatory mechanism. Therefore, the Greer data do not identify the NIS inhibition level that exceeds the body's biological ability to maintain normal thyroid hormone homeostasis. Thus, the perchlorate RfD does not incorporate the effect thyroid hormone homeostasis has on avoiding an adverse effect. Not quantifying the amount that thyroid homeostasis has on avoiding an adverse effect introduces uncertainty into the appropriate value for the perchlorate RfD.

- Uncertainty Introduced by the Small Data Set of the Key Study – The perchlorate RfD was derived from the NOEL observed from the inhibition of iodide uptake by the thyroid in seven humans. The small data set size introduces uncertainty regarding the degree to which the NIS stress levels in Greer test subjects are representative of the entire U.S. population. The small data set in the Greer study introduces considerable uncertainty into the estimation of the perchlorate RfD.

- Uncertainty in Characterizing Thyroid Physiology – A traditional RfD risk assessment is not dependent on having a full understanding of the relevant human physiology. A traditional RfD risk assessment relies on descriptive toxicology, which identifies the external dose that induces the onset of adverse effects. A traditional RfD risk assessment does not specifically identify or characterize all the biological events or steps occurring between exposure and the onset of adverse effects. By analogy, a traditional RfD risk assessment treats human physiology like a "black box" and identifies the input exposure level needed to elicit the onset of adverse effects. The specific biological events occurring within the black box are not necessary to identify the POD and to set an RfD.

However, the traditional RfD risk assessment approach was not followed in the establishment of the perchlorate RfD. The external perchlorate dose that initiates a decrease in the iodide uptake by the thyroid was identified. The inhibition of the iodide uptake by the thyroid is a nonadverse event. The uptake of iodide by the thyroid is the first biological event in the synthesis and use of thyroid hormones in the body. Therefore, the perchlorate RfD risk assessment has not identified or characterized all the biological events after the uptake of iodide that lead to an adverse effect. As such, the perchlorate RfD risk assessment has not attempted to quantify the amount of decrease in the iodide uptake needed to induce the onset of adverse effects in any human population. This introduces uncertainty into the establishment of the perchlorate RfD.

An RfD risk assessment attempts to accurately quantify a chronic exposure level for a noncarcinogen that is without adverse effect in humans. However, as identified above, the traditional RfD risk assessment approach used for perchlorate includes numerous sources of uncertainty and variability whose magnitude of effect on the numerical value of the perchlorate RfD is not defined. EPA's own RfD risk assessment guidance states that most toxicologists understand that the traditional RfD risk assessment approach (i.e., FDA's ADI or EPA's RfD) is a "relatively crude estimate of a level of chronic exposure which is not likely to result in adverse effects in humans" (Barnes 1988; EPA 1993, section 1.2.2.2.2). EPA should provide leadership in the development and implementation of new RfD risk assessment approaches that reduce the uncertainty and variability in the RfD derivation, thereby, increasing the confidence and certainty in the RfD's accuracy.

EPA applies uncertainty factors (UF) to account for the scientific uncertainty in the traditional RfD risk assessment approach. However, the NAS Committee states that "no absolute rules exist for application of the [uncertainty] factors, and professional judgment is a large component of their use" (NAS 2005, p 29). Since the amount of scientific uncertainty is not specifically quantified in a traditional RfD risk assessment, the total amount of UFs needed to account for the scientific uncertainty cannot be independently verified or validated. Therefore, the total amount of UFs applied in a traditional RfD risk assessment is a subjective process left to the professional judgment of scientists. Since any particular group of scientists has an array of opinions on the amount of scientific uncertainty in the chemical dataset, the consensus process of selecting an appropriate amount of UFs to apply is argumentative and rather unscientific. By contrast, the use of quantitative dose-response models is desirable because the scientific uncertainty contributed by a confounding variable is specifically quantified and accounted for when identifying the exposure level that induces the onset of adverse effects. Therefore, a dose-response model reduces the overall scientific uncertainty in a risk assessment and allows the uncertainty contributed by a confounding variable to be objectively evaluated and verified.

EPA uses the risk assessment method originally developed in 1954 to derive the perchlorate RfD. The original Lehman and Fitzhugh Model derived an ADI (i.e., renamed RfD by EPA) by applying a 10-fold safety factor (i.e., later renamed to uncertainty factor (UF) by EPA) to the NOAEL to allow for human variability (Dorne 2005, p 21). EPA's perchlorate RfD was derived by applying a 10-fold uncertainty to the POD to allow for human variability. EPA, using the same basic 56-year-old risk assessment method that Lehman and Fitzhugh developed in 1954 to derive the perchlorate RfD, does not take advantage of current advances in science and technology. ORD's *Strategic Plan for Evaluating the Toxicity of Chemicals* indicates that the implementation of the new science paradigm will take another 10 to 20 years (EPA 2009, p 23). Taking 66 to 76 years to substantially improve the risk assessment process is a poor reflection on both the risk assessment community and the scientific profession of toxicology. Furthermore, it was initially recommended that ORD improve risk assessments by implementing cumulative risk assessments 18 years ago; the recommendation to implement quantitative, mechanistic dose-response models was made 16 years ago. Technology and scientific data exist now to implement cumulative risk assessments and quantitative, mechanistic dose-response models on a select number of well studied chemicals. Waiting an additional 10 to 20 years for ORD to implement the new science paradigm is unacceptable because public health is put at risk and limited environmental resources expended on potentially unnecessary clean-ups are wasted. The risk assessment community must be more open to the development, use, evaluation, and validation of new risk assessment techniques.

Uncertainty and Variability in the Cumulative Risk Assessment

EPA ORD comments that in its opinion, the use of *in vitro* data is premature and may increase the overall uncertainty in the cumulative risk assessment. Therefore, this section compares how the OIG cumulative risk assessment addresses the principal sources of scientific uncertainty and variability observed in the traditional risk assessment approach used to set the perchlorate RfD.

The critical aspect of the OIG cumulative risk assessment approach is the evaluation of the dose-response relationship between the total NIS stress level and the onset of adverse effects in humans. Establishing the dose-response relationship between exposure and adverse effects is a fundamental aspect of toxicity testing. However, as applied to the uptake of iodide by the thyroid, the exposure to a single NIS stressor (e.g., perchlorate) is not adequate to define the total NIS stress level on the thyroid. EPA risk assessment guidance instructs the risk assessor to aggregate the risk from multiple chemicals or stressors sharing the same mechanism of toxicity. Since thiocyanate, nitrate, perchlorate, and the lack of iodide act through the same mechanism of toxicity, the combined biological NIS stress acting on the thyroid from all four NIS stressors represents the exposure level. The total NIS stress acting on the thyroid from concurrent exposure to all four NIS stressors is measured by the total iodide uptake (TIU) level. A lower TIU value represents more environmental stress acting on the thyroid. In the OIG cumulative risk assessment, the TIU is the measurement of exposure. The TIU is the measurement of how perturbed the biological step of iodide uptake has become in the thyroid as result of the combined exposure to all four NIS stressors. By establishing the dose-response relationship between the total NIS stress level (i.e., measured by TIU) and the onset of adverse effects in humans, the OIG cumulative risk assessment greatly reduces the uncertainty and variability in the risk assessment.

The OIG cumulative risk assessment reduces the uncertainty in the risk characterization of perchlorate toxicity by implementing several recommendations for improving risk assessments for reducing uncertainty. The OIG cumulative risk assessment implements the following four recommendations:

1) Since 1992, NAS and other risk assessment experts have recommended the development and implementation of cumulative risk assessments on chemicals sharing the same mechanism of toxicity.

2) Since 1994, NAS and other risk assessment experts have recommended the use of quantitative, mechanistic dose-response modeling to better characterize chemical toxicity, thereby allowing the implementation of predictive risk assessments.

3) In 1994, NAS issued *Science and Judgment in Risk Assessment,* which specifically recommends that EPA reduce the uncertainty by using PBPK models to improve the measurement of exposure by identifying and using the chemical dose actually reaching the target tissue.

4) In 2008, NAS issued *Science and Decisions: Advancing Risk Assessment,* which recommended that EPA " . . . incorporate interactions between chemical and nonchemical stressors in [risk] assessments" (NAS 2008, exec. sum., p 9). Dietary iodide is a nonchemical NIS stressor whose exposure level directly alters the occurrence and onset of adverse effects in humans.

The following discusses how the OIG cumulative risk assessment addresses the principal sources of scientific uncertainty and variability identified in the traditional risk assessment approach used to set the EPA perchlorate RfD:

- Uncertainty in the Biological Response to a Low Uptake of Iodide – The NAS Committee proposed that hypothyroidism would be the first adverse effect observed in humans from an inadequate iodide uptake from excessive perchlorate exposure (NAS 2005, p 166). However, the OIG cumulative risk assessment identified in the scientific literature that a less-severe thyroid condition called hypothyroxinemia is the first adverse effect from a low TIU (Obregon 2005). Hypothyroxinemia is a less-severe thyroid condition than hypothyroidism. Hypothyroxinemia is characterized by a decrease in the T_4 serum level and a normal or slightly elevated T_3 level, without an increase in TSH levels. Low maternal TIU is the most widespread cause of maternal hypothyroxinemia. Although hypothyroxinemia is not a permanent adverse effect in adults (i.e., it is reversible), hypothyroxinemia in the first 20 weeks of pregnancy is associated with permanent mental deficits and an increased frequency of attention-deficit/hyperactivity disorder (ADHD) in their children (Vermiglio 1994).

Identifying and observing an adverse effect from exposure is a fundamental and defining characteristic of an environmental risk assessment. Therefore, identifying the first adverse biological response to a low TIU and then observing its occurrence in the human population from exposure to the NIS stressors reduces the amount of uncertainty and increases the confidence in the cumulative risk assessment.

- Uncertainty in Detecting Adverse Effects in Adults – Unlike the traditional risk assessment approach used for the perchlorate RfD, the OIG cumulative risk assessment specifically observes adverse effects in humans from the total NIS stress load acting on the thyroid. The total NIS stress load is measured in %TIU where a low %TIU indicates a higher NIS stress load. The OIG cumulative risk assessment identified that the more severe thyroid condition of hypothyroidism is reported in humans at a TIU level of about 13.3%. The less severe thyroid condition of hypothyroxinemia is observed in men, women, and pregnant women at TIU levels of about 18%, 22.7%, and 24.5%, respectively. Although hypothyroidism or hypothyroxinemia cannot be measured directly in fetal thyroids, onset of adverse effects from exposure to excessive gestational NIS stress can be detected in the offspring of mothers with maternal TIU levels up to 49%. Therefore, observing adverse effects in adults from exposure to excess NIS stress allows for a proper environmental risk assessment where the relationship between the exposure level and the onset of adverse effects is clearly defined. Identifying the exposure level that induces the first adverse effect in adults reduces the uncertainty and increases the confidence in the cumulative risk assessment approach.

- Uncertainty in Identifying Adverse Effects from NIS Stress during Gestation – Unlike the traditional risk assessment approach used for the perchlorate RfD, the OIG cumulative risk assessment specifically identifies the adverse effects in children from exposure to excessive gestational NIS stress. Since the fetal NIS stress level cannot be measured directly, the OIG cumulative risk assessment uses the maternal NIS stress level as a substitute measure for the fetal NIS stress level. The OIG cumulative risk assessment identified that a maternal NIS stress level within the range of 24.5% to 49% TIU is associate with the following mild adverse effects in her child: delayed reaction time and increased frequency of mild thyroid dysfunction in childhood. The OIG cumulative risk assessment found that further increasing the maternal NIS stress level to the range of 10% to 24.5% TIU is associated with the following moderate adverse effects in her child: lower verbal intelligence quotient (IQ), lower overall IQ, lower motor performance, and increased occurrence of ADHD. Finally, the extreme maternal NIS stress level below 10% TIU is associated with severe adverse effects of cretinism (i.e., severe and permanent mental and physical deficits), which are known to occur at a rate of 5% to 15% at this level of maternal NIS stress. Therefore, by specifically identifying the resulting adverse effects from exposure to excessive gestational NIS stress, the OIG cumulative risk assessment has substantially improved the risk characterization of the public health risk occurring during low maternal TIU. This improves the risk characterization and decreases the uncertainty in the cumulative risk assessment.

- Uncertainty in Dose-response in the Most Sensitive Population – The dose-response curve is a fundamental element in characterizing the toxicity of a chemical. Unlike the traditional risk assessment approach, which did not identify a dose response in the most sensitive population (i.e., the fetus), the OIG cumulative risk assessment did identify a dose-response relationship in the most sensitive population (see section 8.2 of the *OIG Scientific Analysis of Perchlorate* for more details). The dose-response relationship between increasing maternal NIS stress level (i.e., a surrogate measure for the fetal NIS stress level) results in an increased occurrence and severity of adverse effects in her offspring, as summarized in the following table:

Dose: Total NIS Stress Level During Pregnancy (%TIU)*	Adverse Effects Observed in Children Exposed to Excessive NIS Stress During Gestation
49% to 245%	No increased occurrence of mental or physical effects
24.5% to 49%	Delayed reaction time Increased frequency of mild thyroid dysfunction in childhood
10% to 24.5%	Lower verbal intelligence quotient (IQ) Lower overall IQ Lower motor performance Increased occurrence of ADHD
< 10% TIU	Cretinism 5–15% prevalence (severe, permanent mental and physical defects)

* A lower %TIU value represents a greater NIS stress level acting on the thyroid. A 100% TIU level represents exposure conditions in which a normal amount of iodide is being taken up by the thyroid. By comparison, a 10% TIU level represents exposure conditions in which only 10% of the normal amount of iodide is being taken up by the thyroid.

Source: OIG Analysis, summary of adverse effects.

Therefore, the OIG cumulative risk assessment identifies a dose-response relationship between the maternal NIS stress level and the occurrence and severity of adverse effects in her offspring. The identification of a dose-response relationship reduces the uncertainty in the cumulative risk assessment.

- Variability in Measuring Exposure – External dose is a poor measure of actual exposure levels within the body at the site of injury. In 1994, NAS issued *Science and Judgment in Risk Assessment,* which specifically recommends that EPA incorporate PBPK models into environmental risk assessments to identify the dose reaching the target tissue (i.e., the biologically effective dose) (NAS 1994, p 10). For perchlorate exposure, the relationship between external dose and internal dose at the target tissue is not linear. At low external perchlorate doses, the relative internal dose increases (Clewell 2007, p 423, table 4). Furthermore, an external perchlorate dose generates different internal serum concentrations depending on the life stage (i.e., adult, fetus, neonate, child, pregnant women, and nursing women), (Clewell 2007, p 423, table 4). The OIG cumulative risk assessment reduces this uncertainty in measuring dose by using the Clewell PBPK Model for determining the internal perchlorate serum concentration.

- Uncertainty in the Measuring the POD in the Sensitive Populations- In the Greer study, the POD was identified in adult males and females. However, the most sensitive population is developing fetuses during pregnancy (NAS 2005, p 27). Therefore, the POD used was not determined in the most sensitive population, which introduces scientific uncertainty into the traditional risk assessment. However, the OIG cumulative risk assessment does not have this uncertainty because both the LOAEL POD and NOAEL POD were identified for the most sensitive population, fetuses.

- Uncertainty in the Perchlorate RfD as a Function of Dietary Iodide Intake - The NAS Committee stated that the "primary source of uncertainty" arises from the absence of data on possible effects from perchlorate in pregnant women, their fetuses, and newborns with iodide deficiency (NAS 2005, p 18). However, the traditional single chemical risk assessment approach does not attempt to quantify the effect that dietary iodide intake has on the body's ability to tolerate NIS inhibition. Therefore, dietary iodide intake introduces the primary source of scientific uncertainty into the establishment of the perchlorate RfD value.

  The OIG directly addresses this primary source of scientific uncertainty into the establishment of the perchlorate RfD value by directly incorporating dietary iodide into the OIG cumulative risk assessment. The OIG NIS dose-response model uses the iodide dietary level as one of the four exposure variables used to calculate the NIS stress load acting on the thyroid. However, incorporating dietary iodide intake into the OIG cumulative risk assessment has substantially reduced the uncertainty introduced by dietary iodide intake on the perchlorate risk assessment.

- Variability in the Perchlorate RfD as a Function of Body's Goitrogen Load - Perchlorate exposure alone is a poor indicator of the total amount of NIS stress acting on the thyroid. Thiocyanate and nitrate also act as NIS inhibitors to block the uptake of iodide by the thyroid. EPA risk assessment guidance specifically instructs risk assessors to aggregate the risk from chemicals that share the same mechanism of toxicity and elicit the same effect (EPA 1986; EPA 2000).

  The OIG directly addresses this source of variability in the perchlorate RfD value by directly incorporating the exposure to all three NIS inhibitors into the OIG cumulative risk assessment. The OIG NIS dose-response model uses the exposure to the three NIS inhibitors as three of the four exposure variables used to calculate the total NIS stress load acting on the thyroid. Therefore, by using the exposure from all three NIS inhibitors to calculate the total NIS stress level acting on the thyroid, the OIG cumulative risk assessment has substantially reduced this variability within the perchlorate risk assessment.

- Uncertainty in Incorporating Homeostasis - The Greer study measured the thyroid's short-term response to NIS inhibition. The Greer study did not evaluate the thyroid's biological ability to adapt to changes in NIS inhibition levels or the developing brain's biological ability to adapt to a decreased supply of T_4 hormone through the activation of brain's D2-D3 deiodinase compensatory mechanism.

  The OIG cumulative risk assessment is not affected by this uncertainty. The LOAEL POD and NOAEL POD were identified in study populations with chronic exposure to an elevated NIS stress level (e.g., pregnancy occurring in areas of chronic mild or moderate iodide deficiency). Since the OIG cumulative risk assessment relied on the occurrence of adverse effects in the most sensitive population, the chronic exposure to elevated NIS stress levels during gestation has to fully exhaust both the maternal and fetal thyroid's homeostasis and the fetal brain's D2-D3 deiodinase compensatory mechanism before adverse effects appear.

- Uncertainty Introduced by the Small Database Size of the Key Study – The development of the OIG cumulative risk assessment did not rely on a single key study with a small number of test subjects. The OIG used multiple studies of various database sizes to identify the LOAEL POD and NOAEL POD (see section 8.1 and 8.2 of the *OIG Scientific Analysis of Perchlorate* for more details). The OIG cumulative risk assessment used a total of eight studies to identify the LOAEL POD and NOAEL POD, which contained the following number of exposed test subjects: 16, 30, 52, 56, 162, 384, 719, and 719. Therefore, the OIG cumulative risk assessment incorporates less uncertainty from this source.

- Uncertainty in Characterizing Thyroid Physiology – A traditional RfD risk assessment is not dependent on having a full understanding of the relevant human physiology. A traditional RfD risk assessment relies on descriptive toxicology that identifies the external dose that induces the onset of adverse effects. Although not specifically known or characterized, a traditional RfD risk assessment incorporates all the biological events occurring between exposure and the onset of adverse effects.

  The OIG uses same the descriptive toxicology technique to identify the dose that induces the onset of adverse effects. So both the traditional RfD risk assessment approach and the OIG cumulative risk assessment approach evaluate the dose response without specifically identifying or characterizing all the physiological and biological steps occurring between the administration of the dose and the onset of adverse effects. However, the OIG cumulative risk assessment uses the internal dose at the target tissue and not the external dose to establish the dose response. The OIG's use of the internal dose eliminates some of the uncertainty in the technique.

As described above, the OIG cumulative risk assessment has specifically addressed 11 sources of uncertainty or variability found in the traditional risk assessment approach used to derive the perchlorate RfD in order to improve the scientific certainty in the risk characterization of perchlorate. However, EPA ORD states in their comments that the OIG's "use of the *in vitro* NIS data is premature and may increase the overall uncertainty in the cumulative risk assessment." However, ORD does not provide a reasoned explanation for their opinion that the uncertainty in the OIG cumulative risk assessment may have increased. To the contrary, the OIG has specifically identified 11 sources of uncertainty or variability found in the traditional risk assessment approach used to derive the perchlorate RfD and has described how the OIG cumulative risk assessment has reduced these uncertainties. Furthermore, the OIG cumulative risk assessment implements four NAS recommendations for improving the scientific certainty of an environment risk assessment. Therefore, ORD's claim that the uncertainty in the OIG cumulative risk assessment may have increased is not well supported.

In 1994, NAS issued *Science and Judgment in Risk Assessment,* which specifically states, "As scientific knowledge increases, the science policy choices made by the agency and Congress should have less impact on regulatory decision-making. Better data and increased understanding of biological mechanisms should enable risk assessments that are less dependent on conservative default assumptions [e.g., use of uncertainty factors] and more accurate as predictions of human risk" (NAS 1994, p 6). The OIG cumulative risk assessment represents an increased understanding of the biological mechanism of iodide uptake by the NIS because it specifically identifies the NIS stress exposure levels (i.e., high and low exposure levels) that induce adverse effects in the most sensitive human population. With this level of information on toxicity, the conventional application of UFs is not warranted. Furthermore, the dose-response relationship of NIS stress is U-shaped (i.e., too much or too little NIS stress can induce adverse effects) so that the conventional application of UFs cannot be applied, even if desired, to establish a safety margin. The OIG cumulative risk assessment identified that a maternal NIS stress level must be maintained within the range of 49% to 245% TIU to avoid adverse effects in the most sensitive population. The OIG cumulative risk assessment applied an unconventional 1.5 UF to the %$TIU_{(NOAEL)}$ of 49% to generate a %$TIU_{(RfD)}$ of 74%, to generate a small safety margin for the left side of the U-shaped curve.

In short, the OIG reduces the uncertainty in the risk characterization of perchlorate by incorporating the occurrence of adverse effects, the mechanism of toxicity, and the exposure data from all four NIS stressors into a cumulative, quantitative, mechanistic, NIS dose-response model. The NIS dose-response model provides a better scientific explanation of perchlorate toxicity than the traditional single chemical risk assessment approach. The NIS dose-response model identifies the types of adverse effects that will occur in adult males and females, pregnant women, and children from gestational exposure at several NIS stress levels. With this information, the NIS dose-response model can predict the type and the occurrence of adverse effects in a population given the exposure level to each of the four NIS stressors.

Corroboration and Verification of the OIG Cumulative Risk Assessment

The corroboration and verification of the OIG cumulative risk assessment is constrained by the available studies in the scientific literature with suitable study designs. The OIG cumulative risk assessment is based on a mechanistic dose-response model of the iodide uptake by the thyroid from the concurrent exposure to all four NIS stressors. Developing and evaluating this model requires that the internal serum concentrations of the three NIS inhibitors and the iodide nutritional level be measured by the study or be reasonably estimated after the study. This information is needed to determine the total NIS stress level acting on the thyroid (i.e., the "dose" from all four NIS stressors acting on the thyroid). Since perchlorate has a well-developed PBPK model, the internal perchlorate serum concentrations can be estimated from the external perchlorate dose. However, since no PBPK model exist for thiocyanate and nitrate to allow for the estimation of their internal serum concentrations from external exposure, a suitable study would ideally measure both thiocyanate and nitrate serum concentrations. Furthermore, a suitable study also should measure the iodide intake or excretion level of the test subjects. A study rarely measures and reports the test subjects exposure to all four NIS stressors. Therefore, the OIG corroborated and verified the cumulative risk assessment with the best available studies in the scientific literature with suitable study designs.

The scientific merit of the *OIG Scientific Analysis of Perchlorate* should be evaluated by the degree to which the cumulative risk assessment explains and predicts the occurrence of adverse and nonadverse effects in humans. The following summarizes the OIG's corroboration and verification of the OIG cumulative risk assessment (see Section 9.1 of the *OIG Scientific Analysis of Perchlorate* for more details):

- Corroboration of Predicted TIU Levels with Measured TIU Levels in Humans – The OIG cumulative risk assessment uses the *in vitro* NIS Model of Competitive Inhibition to predict the measured TIU levels observed in humans from their exposure to the four NIS stressors. The model's predicted TIU levels are within the statistical variation of the measured TIU levels observed in humans from both the Greer study and the Braverman occupational exposure study (see Sections 9.1.4 and 9.1.5 of the *OIG Scientific Analysis of Perchlorate*).

  The ability of the *in vitro* NIS Model of Competitive Inhibition to accurately predict the measured TIU levels observed in humans provides independent confirmation that the relative potency factors used for the four NIS stressors are correct and applicable to actual human *in vivo* exposures. Furthermore, this agreement between the predicted and measured TIU values validates the use of the predicted TIU as a single exposure parameter, which represents the total NIS stress level acting on the thyroid. By establishing a single exposure parameter, the dose-response relationship can be determined. In the OIG cumulative risk assessment, the dose is the TIU level, which is mathematically derived from the exposure level to each of the four NIS stressors.

- Corroboration of Iodide Uptake as a Nonadverse Effect – The NAS Committee specifically identifies the inhibition of iodide uptake as a non-adverse effect (i.e.,

(NOEL)). In the Greer study, the iodide uptake of individual test subjects was observed to vary as much as ± 55% in the 29-day period between baseline (i.e., point BV) and 15 days post exposure (i.e., point p15) without inducing abnormal thyroid hormone or TSH levels (Greer 2002). Furthermore, in the Braverman occupational exposure study, the perchlorate production workers were measured to have a 38% reduction in iodide uptake without inducing abnormal thyroid hormone or TSH levels (Braverman 2005). Therefore, thyroid homeostasis can accommodate changes in iodide uptake in an adult of at least ± 55% without adversely effecting the normal production and adequate supply of thyroid hormones to the body. The iodide uptake reduction of 1.8% observed at the perchlorate NOEL (73 FR 60262) represents the perchlorate exposure level that induces only a statistically detectable change in iodide uptake levels without a statistically significant change in thyroid hormones or TSH levels. The iodide uptake reduction level required to induce an adverse effect in humans (e.g., abnormal free thyroxine (fT_4) thyroid hormone level) is not identified in either the Greer or Braverman studies. However, the Greer study suggests the iodide uptake would have to be reduced by more than 55% to induce an abnormal thyroid hormone level.

- Hypothyroidism Occurs at a Lower TIU Level Than Hypothyroxinemia – Since hypothyroidism is a more severe thyroid condition than hypothyroxinemia, a greater NIS stress level would be necessary to induce hypothyroidism than hypothyroxinemia (i.e., a lower TIU value represents a higher NIS stress level). Hypothyroidism is reported in humans at a TIU level equivalent to about 13.3%. The OIG cumulative risk assessment identified that hypothyroxinemia is observed in humans at a TIU level of about 18% and 22.7% in men and women, respectively. Therefore, the OIG cumulative risk assessment finding that hypothyroxinemia occurs at a higher TIU level (i.e., representing less NIS stress level) than that required to induce hypothyroidism is consistent with the known severity of these two thyroid conditions.

- Confirmation of the Iodide Uptake Reduction Level Required to Induce the First Adverse Effect – The OIG cumulative risk assessment identified that the first adverse effect, hypothyroxinemia, is not observed until the iodide uptake is reduced over several months by about 82.0%, 77.3 %, and 75.5% in men, women, and pregnant women, respectively. This is consistent with the findings of the scientific expert on the NAS Committee, who stated that "to cause declines in thyroid hormone production that would have adverse health effects, iodide uptake would most likely have to be reduced by at least 75% for months or longer" (NAS 2005, p 8).

- Confirmation of Life-stage Sensitivities to NIS Stress Level - The NAS Committee identifies pregnant women as a sensitive population (NAS 2005, p 18), and the fetus as the most sensitive population (NAS 2005, p 27). Adult men and women can tolerate NIS stress levels up to 18% and 22.7% TIU, respectively, before the onset of hypothyroxinemia. However, the additional demand on the maternal thyroid to supply thyroid hormones to the developing fetus makes pregnant women tolerate less NIS stress than either an adult male or nonpregnant female. The pregnant woman's increased sensitivity to NIS stress is documented in the OIG cumulative risk assessment by an NIS stress level of 24.5% TIU, inducing the onset of hypothyroxinemia. Furthermore, since the immature fetal thyroid is unable to increase its avidity for iodide (Delange 2005a), the fetus is more vulnerable to increased NIS stress than pregnant women or adults. Although the fetal hypothyroxinemia cannot be directly measured *in vivo*, the increased fetal sensitivity to NIS stress is identified by the occurrence of mild adverse effects in childhood of fetuses born to mothers with NIS stress levels up to 49% TIU. Therefore, the OIG cumulative risk assessment confirms that pregnant women are more sensitive than adults to NIS stress and that fetuses are the more sensitive to NIS stress than either pregnant women or adults.

- Confirmation of Dose Additivity - Since 1986, EPA has assumed that the toxicity of individual chemicals in a chemical mixture add together (i.e., dose additivity) when the chemicals have the same mechanism of toxicity, elicit the same effects, and act as dilutions of one another. As applied to this public health issue, the same NIS stress level of about 23% is observed to induce the same adverse effect, hypothyroxinemia, in women, regardless of whether the increased NIS stress is caused by excess exposure to the lack of iodide or by an excess exposure to thiocyanate. In the OIG cumulative risk assessment, we demonstrated that the increased NIS stress from the lack of iodide under a normal goitrogen load induced maternal hypothyroxinemia at a total NIS stress level of about 24.5% TIU. Furthermore, we also demonstrated that the increased NIS stress from excess thiocyanate exposure under a normal iodide intake induced the same adverse effect, hypothyroxinemia, in adult women, at approximately the same total NIS stress level of about 22.7% TIU. Therefore, this information provides direct confirmation that dose additivity occurs between the lack of iodide and thiocyanate stressors.

- Dose-response Relationship – The OIG cumulative risk assessment identifies a dose-response relationship between the maternal NIS stress level (i.e., the dose) and the increasing severity and frequency of adverse effects in her offspring (i.e., the response), (see Section 8.2 of the *OIG Scientific Analysis of Perchlorate* for more details). For example, a maternal NIS stress level within the range of 49% to 245% TIU is not associated with adverse effects. However, increasing the maternal NIS stress level within the range of 24.5% to 49% TIU, the mild adverse effects of delayed reaction time and increased frequency of mild thyroid dysfunction in childhood have been detected in this group of offspring. A further increase in the maternal NIS stress level within the range of 10% to 24.5% TIU results in moderate adverse effects of lower verbal IQ, lower overall IQ, lower motor performance, and increased occurrence of ADHD observed in this group of offspring. Finally, increasing the maternal NIS stress level below 10% results in the severe adverse effects of cretinism (i.e., severe and permanent mental and physical deficits) at a rate of 5% to 15% in this group of offspring. Therefore, the

OIG cumulative risk assessment identifies a dose-response relationship between the maternal NIS stress level and the occurrence and severity of adverse effects in her offspring. The establishment of a dose-response relationship is one of the principal elements in establishing cause and effect.

Predictive Risk Assessment

EPA's Strategic Plan for Evaluating the Toxicity of Chemicals (EPA 2009) states that using "data from subcellular or cell-based *in vitro* assays" to quantitatively characterize the perturbation of the biological process can be used to conduct a "predictive risk assessment" (EPA 2009, p 8). The OIG cumulative risk assessment can be corroborated and validated by evaluating its ability to predict the public health risk from exposure to NIS stressors. As a quantitative, mechanistic NIS dose-response model, the OIG cumulative risk assessment can be used to predict the potential occurrence of an adverse effect for a given NIS stress level (i.e., the dose) in a study population. Conversely, the OIG cumulative risk assessment can be used to predict the NIS stress level needed to induce an adverse effect in a study population. Although the total NIS stress level needed to induce an adverse effect is identified in the NIS dose-response model, the exposures levels to each of the four NIS stressors can vary independently with each study population. For example, the NIS dose-response model can estimate the exposure level from one NIS stressor that is needed to induce an adverse effect in a study population given the exposure level to the other three NIS stressors.

To provide addition corroboration for the OIG cumulative risk assessment, the OIG's NIS dose-response model will predict the potential occurrence of an adverse effect for the NIS stress level (i.e., the dose) in each of the following two study populations (Note: The following two studies were not used by the OIG during the development or initial corroboration of the OIG cumulative risk assessment):

- In the suburbs of Ramat Hasharon, Israel, the population is exposed to perchlorate in the drinking water at concentrations up to 340 ug/L (Amitai 2007). Blood samples were collected from the newborns within 36 to 48 hours of birth. The mean T_4 values measured in the neonates from the very high exposure group (i.e., perchlorate drinking water concentration up to 340 ug/L) and the control group (i.e., perchlorate drinking water concentration less than 3 ug/L) were 13.9 ± 3.8ug/dL, and 14.0 ± 3.5ug/dL, respectively.

  The OIG cumulative risk assessment can provide a quantitative explanation of why the maternal consumption of contaminated drinking water containing up to 340 ug/L of perchlorate does not provide a sufficient amount of additional NIS stress to induce adverse effects in her offspring. In a 70-kg pregnant woman, the consumption of 2 liters of contaminated drinking water containing up to 340 ug/L of perchlorate corresponds to an intake of about 0.01 mg/kg-day (i.e., 340 ug/L x 0.001 mg/ug x 2 liters per day ÷ 70 kg). Using the Clewell PBPK Model, the model predicts a serum concentration of 0.04 mg/L in a pregnant woman from the external dose of 0.01 mg/kg-day of perchlorate (Clewell 2007, p 423, table 4). An estimated serum concentration of 0.04 mg/L converts to a perchlorate serum concentration of 0.4 umol/L. (Note: By comparison, the study measures the perchlorate blood level in a proxy group and found it to be 0.006 mg/L. Our estimated serum concentration of 0.04 mg/L represents the maximum possible perchlorate serum concentration from always drinking the most contaminated water at 340 ug/L, not the average level of contamination level for the group.) The additional perchlorate intake of 680 ug/day increases the body's total NIS inhibition load from the normal level of 1.501 umol/L to 1.901 umol/L.

The Israel study did not measure the iodide nutrition level, but the study was conducted in an iodide-sufficient area. Studies that do not measure the iodide nutrition level in the test subjects introduce a considerable amount of uncertainty into the estimation of the test subjects' total NIS stress level. However, assuming the pregnant women in this study have a normal iodide nutritional level, the Tonacchera Model estimates a TIU of 0.3204x for a total NIS inhibition load of 1.901 umol/L in pregnant women at a normal iodide intake level. Using the typical NIS stress level in the U.S. population of 0.3675x, we estimate the NIS stress level in these pregnant women at 87.0%TIU (i.e., %TIU = (0.3204x ÷ 0.3675x) x 100%) According to the OIG NIS dose-response model, an NIS stress level in pregnant women at or below 49% TIU is needed to induce the onset of mild adverse effects (i.e., such as delayed reaction time and increased frequency of mild thyroid dysfunction in childhood) in their offspring. Furthermore, according to the OIG NIS dose-response model, an NIS stress level in pregnant women at or below 24.5% TIU is needed to induce the onset of moderate adverse effects (i.e., such as lower verbal IQ, lower overall IQ, lower motor performance, and increased occurrence of ADHD in their offspring.

The OIG NIS dose-response model estimates the maximum NIS stress level observed in pregnant women consuming perchlorate-contaminated drinking up to 340 ug/L would be 87% TIU. Reminder: Higher %TIU values represent a lower NIS stress level. Since the estimated maximum NIS stress level in these pregnant women is above the %TIU$_{(NOAEL)}$ in pregnant women of 49%, the findings from the OIG cumulative risk assessment predict that no adverse effects should be observed in their children. Furthermore, since the estimated maximum NIS stress level in these pregnant women is also above the %TIU$_{(RfD)}$ in pregnant women of 74%, the findings from the OIG cumulative risk assessment predict that no adverse effects should be observed in their children with a comfortable margin of safety. The OIG cumulative risk assessment prediction is consistent with this study's reported findings that no significant change was observed in neonate T_4 values, birth weight, or gestational age between the very high exposure group (i.e., perchlorate drinking water conc. up to 340 ug/L) and the control group (i.e., perchlorate drinking water conc. less than 3 ug/L). Although neonate T_4 values, birth weight, and gestational age are not the best indicators for detecting adverse effects in children from the potential exposure to excessive NIS stress during pregnancy, the use of these indicators is not surprising because the specific adverse effects from excessive exposure to NIS stress during pregnancy had not been identified by the OIG until after this Israel study had been conducted.

- In 1984, a group of patients with hyperthyroidism caused by Graves' disease were treated with perchlorate (NAS 2005, p 61; Wenzel 1984). For the first year, 18 patients were treated initially with 900 mg per day. As serum thyroid hormone concentrations declined, the dose of potassium perchlorate was reduced to an average of 93 mg/day (i.e., 93,000 ug/day) for the second year. During the second year, all the patients had normal serum T_4 and T_3 concentrations, and the majority had normal serum concentrations of TSH-receptor-stimulating antibodies, the cause of hyperthyroidism in patients who had Graves' disease; this indicated that they no longer had Graves' disease (i.e., conceptually, the patients during the second year had a normally functioning thyroid). The NAS Committee states, "Given that most of the patients did not have high serum concentrations of TSH-receptor stimulating antibodies during the second year of perchlorate therapy, the results strongly suggest that moderate doses of perchlorate given chronically do not cause hypothyroidism" (NAS 2005, p 61).

The OIG cumulative risk assessment can provide a quantitative explanation of why the ingestion of 93,000 ug/day of perchlorate does not provide a sufficient amount of additional NIS stress to induce hypothyroidism in an adult. In a 70-kg adult, the ingestion of 93 mg/day of perchlorate corresponds to an intake of 1.33 mg/kg-day. The Clewell PBPK Model predicts a serum concentration of 1.33 mg/L in an adult from the external dose of 1.33 mg/kg-day of perchlorate (Clewell 2007, p 423, table 4). A serum concentration of 1.33 mg/L converts to a perchlorate serum concentration of 13.3 umol/L. The additional perchlorate intake of 93 mg/day increases the body's total NIS inhibition load from the normal level of 1.501 umol/L to 14.8 umol/L. The patients' iodide nutrition level is not identified, which introduces a considerable amount of uncertainty into the estimation of their NIS stress level. However, assuming the patients' average iodide nutritional level is normal, the Tonacchera Model estimates a TIU of 0.0624x for a total NIS inhibition load of 14.8 umol/L at a normal iodide intake level. Since the typical NIS stress level in the U.S. population is 0.3675x, the NIS stress level in these patients is estimated at 17.0% TIU. According to the OIG cumulative risk assessment, an NIS stress level at or below 13.3% TIU is needed to induce hypothyroidism in an adult. Therefore, since the patients' NIS stress level of 17% TIU is above 13.3% TIU needed to induce the onset of hypothyroidism, the findings from the OIG cumulative risk assessment correctly predicts that hypothyroidism would not be observed in these patients.

The confidence in the OIG cumulative risk assessment could be increased by evaluating its ability to accurately predict the occurrence of adverse effects in additional exposure studies of NIS stressors. The OIG sought to identify additional exposure studies that provide suitable data on the exposure levels of the four NIS stressors so that the NIS dose-response model could make a prediction. For balance in the corroboration of the OIG cumulative risk assessment, the OIG specifically sought to find an exposure study in the scientific literature in which the NIS stress level was sufficiently high so that the NIS dose-response model would predict the occurrence of adverse effects. A sufficiently high NIS stress level to induce adverse effects is expected to occur only in areas of endemic cretinism (i.e., areas with high NIS inhibitor exposure accompanied with low iodide intake). Although exposure studies exist in areas of endemic cretinism, the OIG could not identify one with suitable exposure data for all the NIS stressors. These studies often report only iodide excretion levels and thiocyanate consumption data. However, since no PBPK models exist for thiocyanate or nitrate, the NIS dose-response model needs these exposure studies to directly measure the serum concentrations of thiocyanate and nitrate. Furthermore, these exposure studies in areas of endemic cretinism do not measure for perchlorate exposure, because perchlorate exposure is not considered by the medical community to be a significant contributing factor in the etiology of cretinism.

Achieving a "Meaningful Opportunity" for Health Risk Reduction

Section 1412(B)(1) of the 1996 Safe Drinking Water Act Amendments directs EPA to determine whether to regulate a drinking water contaminants with a National Primary Drinking Water Regulation (NPDWR) using the following three criteria:

(a) the contaminant may have an adverse effect on the health of persons;

(b) the contaminant is known to occur or there is substantial likelihood that the contaminant will occur in public water systems with a frequency and at levels of public health concern; and

(c) in the sole judgment of the Administrator, regulation of such contaminant presents a meaningful opportunity for health risk reduction for persons served by public water systems.

If all three statutory criteria are met, EPA makes a determination that an NPDWR is needed for the unregulated drinking water contaminant. If so, the Agency has 24 months to publish a proposed maximum contaminant limit (MCL) and NPDWR. After the proposed NPDWR, the Agency has 18 months to publish a final NPDWR, which sets an EPA drinking water MCL for the contaminant.

The critical judgment in determining the need for an NPDWR is that the potential MCL provides a meaningful opportunity for health risk reduction. In environmental risk management, the goal is to prevent the occurrence of adverse effects in humans with an acceptable margin of safety. The goal of environmental risk management is not to prevent the occurrence of any biological change in the body from exposure to a specific chemical. Conceptually, an exposure level that induces no detectable biological changes within the body is without risk of adverse effects (i.e., an adverse effect is the results of biological changes). EPA's perchlorate RfD and the subsequent health reference level (HRL) used in the regulatory determination-making process is identifying an perchlorate exposure level that will prevent the occurrence of any measurable biological change in the body at all life stages. Although an admirable goal, attempting to avoid all measureable risk from perchlorate exposure is neither practical nor achievable. The NAS Committee states that adverse health effects have not been clearly demonstrated in any human population exposed to perchlorate (NAS 2005, p 177). Because no adverse effects have been observed in the human population from perchlorate exposure, achieving the goal of environmental risk management is already mostly met. The perchlorate RfD and subsequently implemented HRL should incorporate a reasonable margin of safety to protect human health.

EPA's interim perchlorate health advisory (HA) of 15 ug/L issued on January 8, 2009, (EPA 2008a) provides for an ample margin of safety to protect against adverse effects in humans. The margin of safety in EPA's interim perchlorate HA can only be estimated due to the lack of observed adverse effects in humans. In Israel, no adverse effects have been observed in children born to pregnant women consuming perchlorate-contaminated drinking water with up to 340 ug/L (i.e., ppb) of perchlorate (Amitai 2007). Likewise, in Chile, no adverse effects have been observed in children born to pregnant women consuming perchlorate-contaminated drinking water with a mean perchlorate level of 114 ug/L (i.e., ppb) (Tellez 2005; Crump 2000). The Lehman and Fitzhugh Model (i.e., the origin of the traditional risk assessment approach) derives an acceptable exposure level by applying a 10-fold safety factor to the NOAEL to allow for human variability (Dorne 2005, p 21). For simplicity, the OIG is estimating the margin of safety in the perchlorate RfD using the drinking water concentration because the other factors are constant for a given life-stage in a traditional risk assessment (i.e., weight, daily water consumption, thiocyanate exposure, nitrate exposure, and dietary iodide intake level). Since the human NOAEL in drinking water from the Israel study appears to be greater than 340 ug/L, EPA's interim perchlorate HA of 15 ug/L has an estimated margin of safety that is greater than 22.7 times. Likewise, since the human NOAEL in drinking water from the Chilean study is greater than 114 ug/L, EPA's interim perchlorate health advisory of 15 ug/L, with all other factors being equal (i.e., no confounding factors), has an estimated margin of safety greater than 7.6 times. Therefore, using the traditional risk assessment standard of avoiding adverse effects in humans by at least a factor of 10, EPA's interim perchlorate HA of 15 ug/L provides an ample margin of safety to protect against adverse effects in humans.

In its August 19, 2009, Federal Register notice (74 FR 41883), EPA stated it is considering alternate approaches to derive HRLs by reassessing exposure assumptions at different life stages. This reassessment of the HRL is based on infants consuming more perchlorate in their daily food than adults on a per-kg-body-weight basis (Murray 2008, table 5) and on infants consuming more drinking water daily than adults on a per-kg-body-weight basis (74 FR 41883, table 2). Taking these increased exposure assumptions in infants into consideration; EPA is evaluating a perchlorate HRL as low as 1 ug/L for infants between 1 to < 3 months old and at a 95th percentile ingestion rate of drinking water (74 FR 41883, table 2). Although infant exposures were not specifically quantified in the Chilean or Israeli populations, the infants in these populations would have experienced a corresponding increase in their perchlorate dose as compared with an adult due to the same factors of a greater perchlorate exposure from their daily food than adults on a per-kg-body-weight basis and by consuming more drinking water than adults on a per-kg-body-weight basis. However, although the infants in these populations experienced higher perchlorate dosages than adults on a per-kg-body-weight basis, no adverse effects have been observed in the infants from these high-perchlorate-exposed populations.

The difference in estimated perchlorate exposures as a function of life stage has a little practical effect on changing the margin of safety. The margin of safety is a measure of the difference in dosages between the estimated NOAEL drinking water concentration (i.e., ug/L) and the interim perchlorate HA of 15 ug/L for a specific life stage (i.e., typically for an adult). EPA's interim perchlorate HA of 15 ug/ L was based on an relative source contribution (RSC) of 62% for pregnant women (EPA 2008a, p 24). To calculate the margin of safety for another life stage would require the specific exposure dose at both the estimated NOAEL drinking water concentration and at the RfD for that life stage. For example, an infant would have a higher perchlorate exposure dose on a per-kg-body-weight basis at both the estimated NOAEL drinking water concentration (e.g., high dose) and the interim perchlorate HA of 15 ug/L (e.g., low dose). Therefore, since infants would experience an increased perchlorate exposure on a per-kg-body-weight basis at both the high and low dosage points, the increased infant exposure effect offsets each other (i.e., exposure levels are shifted in the same direction at both the high and low dosage level for a given life stage) leaving the margin of safety between the two dosage points relatively unchanged.

EPA's action of potentially lowering the perchlorate HRL increases the margin of safety for avoiding adverse effects in humans. EPA is considering lowering the perchlorate HRLs to as low as 1 ug/L (74 FR 41883, table 2). MassDEP has set a perchlorate drinking water limit of 2 ug/L. An exact margin of safety cannot be calculated due to the lack of observed adverse effects in humans, but a margin of safety can be estimated. Using a potential HRL of 2 ug/L, the estimated margin of safety becomes greater than 170 times based on the no adverse effects observed in the Israel study. Likewise, using a potential HRL of 2 ug/L, the estimated margin of safety becomes greater than 57 times based on the no adverse effects observed in the Chile study. EPA's potential use of an HRL of 2 ug/L instead of the interim perchlorate HA of 15 ug/L would increase the estimated margin of safety from greater than 7.6 to greater than 57 times using the Chilean exposure and from greater than 22.7 to greater than 170 times using the Israeli exposure. The traditional risk assessment standard uses a margin of safety of 10 to avoid exposure that could result in adverse effects in humans. Therefore, EPA's potential use of an HRL of 2 ug/L exceeds the margin of safety necessary to protect against adverse effects in human. Overabundant caution drives the establishment and consideration of an HRL of 2 ug/L for the perchlorate regulatory determination.

Chemical exposures posing a greater risk to public health provide a greater opportunity for health risk reduction. Public health is at the greatest risk when a chemical's exposure level in the U.S. population is sufficiently high to induce adverse effects. Implementing environmental regulations to lower this exposure provides the greatest opportunity for health risk reduction. The effectiveness of an environmental regulation can be evaluated by the amount of decrease in severity or frequency of the adverse effect occurring in the exposed population after the regulation's implementation. The U.S. population is exposed to some chemicals in sufficient quantities to induce adverse effects. For example, EPA estimates that radon exposure causes about 21,000 lung cancer deaths per year (EPA 2009b, p 2). If EPA implemented a regulation that lowered the radon exposure level in the population, its effectiveness could be evaluated by determining the decrease in lung cancer deaths per year. By comparison, the interim perchlorate HA of 15 ug/L results in no adverse health effects and has an ample margin of safety by traditional risk assessment practices. Potentially implementing a perchlorate HRL below 15 ug/L does not decrease the occurrence of adverse effects in the public and only results in a greater margin of safety.

By comparison, correcting iodide deficiency during pregnancy and lactation provides a more meaningful opportunity for health risk reduction than implementing a perchlorate HRL below 15 ug/L. The OIG cumulative risk assessment estimates up to 276,000 infants per year are being harmed annually in the United States by insufficient iodide uptake by the fetal thyroid during pregnancy and lactation. The reduction in adverse effects in a substantial number of children annually is more meaningful than increasing the margin of safety in the perchlorate HRL.

Cancellation of the Second National Academy of Sciences Review of Perchlorate

In January 2009, EPA announced plans to seek a second NAS review of perchlorate, which was to include a review of the OIG's findings. Subsequently, EPA changed its decision and cancelled the planned second NAS review of perchlorate. In the August 19, 2009, Federal Register notice, the EPA states that it "believes that further review by the [NAS] would unnecessarily delay regulatory decision making for perchlorate" (74 FR 41884). Since a NAS peer review takes about 18 months to complete, EPA could have had the second NAS peer review completed by mid-2010. As late as September 23, 2009, EPA issued a Federal Register notice seeking additional comments on EPA's preliminary regulatory determination on perchlorate (74 FR 48541). EPA intends to issue a final regulatory determination as expeditiously as possible following consideration of the comments and information received by the Agency.

In the August 19, 2009, Federal Register notice, EPA does not identify or articulate a public health need for a quick decision on regulatory determination of perchlorate. On January 8, 2009, EPA established an interim perchlorate HA of 15 ug/L (EPA 2008a). Furthermore, on January 8, 2009, EPA issued guidance lowering Superfund's preliminary remediation goal (PRG) from 24.5 ug/L to 15 ug/L (EPA 2009a). EPA's actions of issuing the interim perchlorate HA and the Superfund PRG restricts the acceptable public exposure to perchlorate to a maximum of 15 ug/L. EPA has not identified the potential harm or risk to public health that the 18 months needed to conduct a second NAS review of perchlorate would cause to the regulatory decisionmaking process. To justify the need to rush the regulatory determination decisionmaking for perchlorate, EPA would have to demonstrate with human epidemiological data that one or more of the following is occurring:

- The interim perchlorate HA of 15 ug/L is ineffective and adverse effects are occurring in the human population.

- The margin of safety used in the interim perchlorate HA of 15 ug/L is inadequate to protect the most sensitive population from adverse effects or is noncompliant with EPA risk assessment guidance.

- The interim perchlorate HA of 15 ug/L is noncompliant with EPA risk assessment guidance.

By contrast, the potential harm of rushing a regulatory determination before a consensus on the actual toxicity of perchlorate is achieved within the scientific community is that EPA could issue a strict perchlorate MCL that is exceedingly expensive to implement without any derived benefit to public health. The harm in rushing a regulatory determination is the risk of potentially wasting limited public health resources to reduce perchlorate exposure below 15 ug/L when the available science has not shown that this level of perchlorate exposure poses a public health problem. To the contrary, the cumulative risk assessment of the four principal NIS stressors provides scientific support that exposure to 15 ug/L of perchlorate has a negligible risk of inducing an adverse effect in humans.

A second NAS review of perchlorate is critically needed for the following three reasons:

- To Mitigate Ongoing Public Harm: The OIG cumulative risk assessment estimates up to 276,000 infants per year are being harmed annually in the United States by insufficient iodide uptake by the thyroid during pregnancy and lactation. This public health threat potentially harms one child every 2 minutes. Considering the severity and frequency of potential harm to children, due diligence requires that this public health threat be independently evaluated in a timely manner. A NAS peer review provides for an independent scientific evaluation of the OIG cumulative risk assessment and its findings. If the NAS peer review were to confirm this public health threat, EPA's cancellation of the planned NAS peer review would have delayed by about 18 months any potential government response to alleviate the threat. In human terms, an 18-month delay represents subtle cognitive damage to up to about 400,000 children that could have potentially been prevented or minimized.

  By comparison, EPA's interim perchlorate HA level identifies that a drinking water exposure level of 15 ug/L "is protective of all subpopulations" (EPA 2008a, p 33). Therefore, since no one is known or thought to be harmed by perchlorate exposure at or below 15 ug/L, a potential delay in making a regulatory determination on perchlorate does not put the public at risk for any known adverse effects.

- To Advance the Science of Environmental Risk Assessment: Risk assessment has used the same approach for the last 55 years. The environmental risk assessments must evolve and incorporate the scientific advancements occurring in the biological fields. For the last 18 years, NAS and other expert panels have called on EPA leadership to implement cumulative risk assessments, to implement predictive risk assessments, and to quantify the probability of harm during the establishment of a reference dose for chemicals inducing noncancerous effects. The manner in which these changes should be implemented was identified in the NAS report titled *Toxicity Testing in the Twenty-First Century: A Vision and A Strategy*. In this report, a new science paradigm for improved implementation of environmental risk assessments is described. To implement dramatic changes in the environmental risk assessment process, bold leadership and vision is needed to break away from the status quo approach to make a significant breakthrough and improve the process.

After 18 years of being instructed to implement cumulative risk assessments, ORD has not issued Agency-wide guidance to implement cumulative risk assessment and states that implementing the new risk assessment paradigm could take another 20 years. Furthermore, ORD has neither proposed nor implemented a single cumulative risk assessment. ORD's only experience with potentially implementing a cumulative risk assessment is ORD's tasking NAS with evaluating the potential of conducting a cumulative risk assessment on phthalate esters (EPA 2008a). By comparison, OPP has already successfully implemented several cumulative risk assessments on pesticide residues sharing the same mechanism of toxicity. Therefore, ORD has not applied innovative techniques in the field of environmental risk assessment. By perpetuating the status quo, ORD management generates a professional work environment that is antagonistic to creative thinking and innovation that is critically needed to improve the confidence in and effectiveness of risk assessments.

A second NAS peer review of perchlorate allows for the evaluation of the new science paradigm for environmental risk assessment that prior NAS committees have been requesting from EPA. The OIG cumulative risk assessment allows NAS to evaluate an example of the new science paradigm applied to a specific environmental exposure threat. The potential recommendations from a second NAS peer review of perchlorate are needed to help advance the evolution of environmental risk assessment. A NAS peer review of the OIG cumulative risk assessment provides a mechanism for an independent and impartial evaluation that is further removed from the politics.

- <u>To Facilitate an Interagency Response to Address this Public Health Threat</u>: The sources of risk culminating in potentially adverse outcomes in humans from a low TIU during pregnancy and lactation crosses multiple regulatory authorities. Potential exposure to the three chemicals that act as NIS inhibitors (i.e., thiocyanate, nitrate, and perchlorate) are within EPA's regulatory authority to oversee and manage. However, the level of iodide deficiency during pregnancy and lactation is the primary factor in determining the severity and frequency of adverse effects in humans, and oversight and management of proper iodide nutrition is outside the regulatory authority of EPA. Therefore, involvement of other federal agencies, such as FDA and Institute of Medicine, is needed to prevent iodide deficiency during pregnancy and lactation and thereby avoid adverse effects in humans. A NAS peer review of the OIG cumulative risk assessment and its findings is necessary to properly motivate the various federal agencies to cooperate on this joint public health issue.

In the OW comment to the OIG (see OW comment #6), EPA identifies that iodide nutrition is outside EPA authority and, therefore, that iodide nutritional status should be treated as a constant in the risk assessment. This OW comment avoids the essential biological variable in the characterization of risk from perchlorate exposure. However, this OW comment is not consistent with EPA's prior charge to the perchlorate NAS Committee to "consider the influence of iodide in the diet on the levels at which adverse effects would be observed, especially in sensitive populations" (NAS 2005, p 30). Furthermore, the OW comment is also not consistent with EPA risk assessment guidance and documentation. EPA's *Guidance on Planning and Scoping for Cumulative Risk*

Assessments Part I – Scoping and Planning specifically identifies nutritional status as a stressor in a cumulative risk assessment (EPA 1997c). Furthermore, EPA's *Framework for Cumulative Risk Assessment* identifies the need to incorporate nutrition in a cumulative risk assessment four separate times (EPA 2003, pp 39, 51, 63, 68). Furthermore, section 4.3 of *EPA's Strategic Plan for Evaluating the Toxicity of Chemicals* specifically identifies collecting available data on nutrients and dietary supplements while conducting a quantitative risk assessment (EPA 2009, p 16). Finally, in 2008, NAS issued *Science and Decisions: Advancing Risk Assessment,* which recommended that EPA " . . . incorporate interactions between chemical and nonchemical stressors in [risk] assessments" (NAS 2008, exec. sum., p 9). Therefore, the OW comment that iodide nutrition should not be included as a stressor in an environmental risk assessment is a mistake because EPA charged the NAS Committee to consider iodide nutrition, and EPA's own risk assessment guidance and documentation instructs risk assessors to include nutrition in their risk assessments.

OIG Specific Responses to Each Comment Submitter

Note: ORD's comments were developed, approved, and submitted to us prior to appointment of the ORD Assistant Administrator and EPA Science Advisor.

OIG Response to EPA Office of Research and Development Comments

UNITED STATES ENVIRONMENTAL PROTECTION AGENCY
WASHINGTON, D.C. 20460

March 10, 2009

OFFICE OF
RESEARCH AND DEVELOPMENT

MEMORANDUM

SUBJECT: Response to OIG draft report *Scientific Analysis of Perchlorate: Cumulative Risk Assessment and Public Health Implications* (2008-0010)

FROM: Kevin Teichman
Deputy Assistant Administrator for Science

TO: Eric Lewis
Director of Special Reviews
Office of Inspector General

Thank you for the opportunity to comment on the draft report *Scientific Analysis of Perchlorate: Cumulative Risk Assessment and Public Health Implications*. EPA has put a great deal of effort into evaluating the health effects associated with perchlorate exposure and has undertaken an analysis of the need for regulation of this chemical in groundwater. EPA has also worked with other federal agencies (e.g., FDA, USDA, etc.) as a part of this effort as a member of the Interagency Working Group for Perchlorate. The potential for cumulative exposure to chemicals other than perchlorate that might affect thyroid hormone function is an issue that should not be taken lightly as your report highlights.

Specific OIG Response:

We agree that the evaluation of the public health risk from the potential disruption of normal thyroid hormone function induced by excessive environmental exposure to NIS stressors is a complex public health issue. Both ORD's 2002 draft perchlorate risk assessment (EPA 2002a) and the 2005 NAS Committee report (NAS 2005) applied a traditional single chemical risk assessment approach to characterize the public health risk.

However, we reviewed both the EPA risk assessment guidance and NAS recommendations to improve environmental risk assessment and found the traditional single chemical risk assessment approach to be inadequate to characterize the public health risk from exposure to multiple NIS stressors acting through the same mechanism of action.

Since 1992, EPA has been directed to improve the environmental risk assessment process through the implementation of cumulative risk assessments. However, over the last 18 years, ORD has not proposed, conducted, or implemented any cumulative risk assessments on any class or group of chemicals. Instead of improving the environmental risk assessment process, ORD continues to rely on and issue single chemical risk assessments using the original, outdated risk assessment approach developed by Dr. Lehman and Dr. Fitzhugh in 1954. Since ORD has not implemented previous recommendations to improve environmental risk assessments, we developed and issued the *OIG Scientific Analysis of Perchlorate* to provide an example of a cumulative risk assessment that implements several recommendations to improve the characterization of environmental public health risk through the use of a cumulative risk assessment. We found that the development and use of innovative risk assessment techniques is needed to better characterize and to more effectively address complex public health issues. This assessment is consistent with the vision for ORD of the new EPA Science Advisor, Paul Anastas, when he writes that "scientific and technological innovation is essential to the success of our mission" (EPA 2010).

Several major issues were identified following our review of the document and the accompanying material including:

Use of the *in vitro* Tonacchera et al. (2004) study for relative potency factor determination: The Tonacchera et al. (2004) study is an *in vitro* study that estimated the relative potency of instantaneous sodium-iodide symporter (NIS) inhibition for several compounds in Chinese hamster ovary (CHO) cells. The OIG report uses this study to predict relative potency for use in the cumulative risk assessment. The use of *in vitro* data for this purpose has major limitations. It is widely acknowledged that use of *in vitro* data has limitations related to kinetics and dynamics, i.e., isolated tissue preparation does not necessarily behave similarly to intact *in vivo* systems. EPA has published numerous guidance documents (U.S. EPA, 1986, 1997, 1998, 2000, 2002, 2007a), evaluation criteria (U.S. EPA, 2003), and state-of-the-art assessments for the cumulative risk of the organophosphorus, triazine, chloroacetanalide and N-methyl carbamate pesticide classes (U.S. EPA 2006a,b,c; 2007b). To date, no *in vitro* data have been used to estimate relative potency due to these concerns. EPA believes that use of the *in vitro* NIS data is premature and may increase the overall uncertainty in the cumulative risk assessment.

Specific OIG Response:

Because this comment constitutes ORD's major critique of our science review, we carefully considered this information. We provided a detailed response to this comment in the previous General Overall Response section. The following summarizes the major issues in our response:

- ORD's objection to our use of *in vitro* data directly contradicts their opinion described in *EPA's Strategic Plan for Evaluating the Toxicity of Chemicals* (EPA 2009).

- Although ORD asserts that the limitations of *in vitro* data preclude it from adequately predicting the occurrence of adverse effects and nonadverse effects in humans, ORD has not provided any data or information that disproves or discredits our cumulative risk characterization of this public health issue.

- ORD continues to prefer using the single chemical risk assessment approach to characterize risk that was developed 56 years ago by Dr. Lehman and Dr. Fitzhugh of FDA. We believe the implementation of innovative risk assessment techniques by ORD is long overdue.

- We examined and compared the sources of uncertainty in both a single chemical risk assessment approach and a cumulative risk assessment approach to the risk characterization of this public health issue. Contrary to ORD's opinion, we found the sources of uncertainty in the cumulative risk assessment approach to be less than the single chemical risk assessment approach.

- The scientific merit of our cumulative risk assessment should be evaluated by how well it explains and predicts the occurrence of adverse and nonadverse effects in the human population.

Level of peer review: The technical review by ICF International scientists alone is not a sufficient or sound peer review for this document. Previous perchlorate assessments have been reviewed by international expert panels via EPA's Scientific Advisory Board, or more recently by the National Academy of Sciences. The OIG's report should be subjected to the same level of peer review by experts in the field of perchlorate toxicity, thyroid function and cumulative risk. In addition, the ICF review clearly states that the Tonacchera et al. (2004) study is not sufficient for use in a cumulative risk approach for goitrogens.

Specific OIG Response:

In the *OIG Scientific Analysis of Perchlorate*, we explain that the Agency's peer review policy encourages and expects all scientific and technical information intended to inform or support Agency decisionmaking (i.e., rulemaking) to be peer reviewed. Specifically, "influential scientific information" and "highly influential scientific assessments" should be peer reviewed in accordance with the Agency's *Peer Review Handbook* (EPA 2006). However, since the OIG does not conduct rulemaking (i.e., the OIG does not develop or issue environmental regulations), our science review did not undergo a formal peer review. We called the work conducted by ICF International a technical review. We never characterized is as a peer review. Our purpose was "to get an independent scientific critique of our application of a cumulative risk assessment to this public health issue" before going public with it. ICF International supported the implementation of a cumulative risk assessment, but recommended using the "whole mixture" cumulative risk assessment approach using CDC's epidemiological analysis as opposed to our dose-addition method approach to the cumulative risk assessment. Based on ICF International's technical review, we provided a detailed critique of CDC's epidemiological analysis. As described in Appendix A, our review of CDC's epidemiological analysis concluded that the whole mixture approach to the risk assessment of perchlorate is not sufficiently developed and corroborated to be the basis for developing a perchlorate RfD or as the basis for establishing a potential perchlorate drinking water limit.

Lack of consideration of NHANES data on effects of perchlorate exposure in the population: The conclusions of the report indicate that effects from perchlorate exposure that would be observable in the population would be masked by exposure to thyroid-active compounds in the diet. Consideration has not been given to the results of the Center for Disease Control and Prevention (CDC) epidemiological analysis (Blount et al., 2006) that demonstrated a relationship between low levels of perchlorate exposure and circulating levels of thyroid hormone, even in the presence of other thyroid-active chemicals from the diet.

Specific OIG Response:

ORD alleges that we did not consider CDC's epidemiological analysis of the NHANES data. Contrary to ORD's opinion, the external review draft clearly shows that we specifically considered CDC's epidemiological analysis of the NHANES data. Our external review draft devoted an entire appendix to the consideration of CDC's epidemiological analysis. Our review of the CDC epidemiological analysis generated a comment from CDC (see CDC comment). Apparently, ORD failed to notice and review an entire appendix addressing CDC's epidemiological analysis of the NHANES data.

The potential regulation of perchlorate is a critical environmental decision that has significant social and economic consequences. The regulation of perchlorate could adversely affect $70 billion dollars worth of U.S. agricultural exports (NASDA 2009). When one considers both the agricultural and environmental clean-up costs, the potential regulation of perchlorate represents at least a $70–110+ billion dollar decision. During our science review, ORD committed to conducting a thorough review of our cumulative risk assessment but later cancelled those plans. The potential regulation of perchlorate is a critical environmental decision; therefore, ORD should have conducted a more substantial, critical review of the *OIG Scientific Analysis of Perchlorate (External Review Draft)*. Otherwise, EPA would be making a perchlorate regulatory determination without considering all of the available data, which reflects poorly on the scientific integrity of ORD.

In regard to the quality of CDC's epidemiological analysis, ORD does not challenge, address, or clarify any specific issue the OIG identified in CDC's epidemiological analysis. In December 2008, during the issuance of the external review draft, we identified in Appendix A eight issues concerning the use of CDC's epidemiological data for the evaluation of the human health risk from perchlorate. Our concerns with the

CDC's epidemiological data include the following: the results have not been independently verified or corroborated in any other dataset; the results are not consistent with the identified mechanism of toxicity or the exposure levels of the four NIS stressors; and the statistical significance of the relationship between decreasing total thyroxine (tT_4) with increasing perchlorate exposure in women with low urinary iodide concentration (UIC) is reportedly lost when the UIC is measured as ug/g creatinine instead of ug/L (Lamm 2007). Furthermore, upon receipt of CDC comments, the OIG has expressed additional issues concerning the use of CDC's epidemiological data for the evaluation of the human health risk from perchlorate (see OIG response to CDC's comments).

With this comment, ORD obviously places a lot of scientific significance in CDC's epidemiological analysis. However, EPA actions do not support this opinion. EPA has not used this CDC study, which reports a relationship between decreasing tT_4 with increasing perchlorate exposure in women with low UIC, to derive EPA's perchlorate RfD of 0.0007 mg/kg-day, to set EPA's perchlorate HA of 15 ug/L, or to set OW's HRL of 15 ug/L. As identified in ICF International's briefing to the OIG on its technical review, CDC's epidemiological analysis reportedly indicates significantly greater perchlorate toxicity than that observed in any other human perchlorate exposure study. In science, the significance of an outlying data point must be evaluated within the context of interrupting all the available data. Both ICF International's technical review and this ORD comment appear to exhibit comfort in dismissing the results of all other human perchlorate experience studies, which collectively indicate a much lower toxicity level for perchlorate, in favor of the only uncorroborated perchlorate exposure study that indicates a much greater toxicity level for perchlorate. The act of discarding, without cause, the bulk of human perchlorate experience studies in favor of the one uncorroborated study can be perceived as scientific bias. We stress that the appearance of scientific bias has no legitimate place in the environmental regulatory rulemaking process.

In summary, in our opinion, the issues we have raised about the scientific analysis in the draft report , i.e., (1) the study relied upon to determine relative potency; (2) the level of peer review, and (3) the lack of consideration of the NHANES data, call into question the supporting basis for the recommendations in the report.

At the same time, we will continue to take into account the potential for cumulative risk from exposure to environmental chemicals when planning our agenda for the upcoming years.

Specific OIG Response:

We thoroughly considered each of ORD's comments. The issues raised by ORD are not persuasive. We have provided our basis for our opinion in the detailed response to each ORD comment. We welcome further review and consideration of our responses by the scientific community while EPA continues the decisionmaking process of the regulatory determination on perchlorate.

ORD's attached references citations are not repeated here, but are included in Appendix D.

OIG Response to EPA's Office of Water Comments

UNITED STATES ENVIRONMENTAL PROTECTION AGENCY
WASHINGTON, D.C. 20460

MAR 1 3 2009

OFFICE OF
WATER

MEMORANDUM

SUBJECT: Office of Water Comments on the *OIG Scientific Analysis of Perchlorate - External Review Draft*

FROM: Michael H. Shapiro
Acting Assistant Administrator

TO: Bill Roderick
Deputy Inspector General
Office of Inspector General

These comments supplement comments the Offices of Water (OW) and Research and Development (ORD) previously provided on the discussion draft of the *OIG Scientific Analysis of Perchlorate: Cumulative Risk Assessment and Its Implications on Public Health* (i.e., the audit report and supplemental report) in October 2008. My understanding is that ORD will be providing comments on this External Review Draft under separate cover.

OW continues to have concerns about the OIG report. Generally, the statements of fact derived from reports, policy documents, and the scientific literature are accurate. However, much of the interpretation of these data and policy inputs deviates significantly from standard application or extends the data beyond its practical limits. The approach to data analysis and application communicated in the OIG report is creative, but we believe it overreaches the current state of the science. Our specific concerns are outlined below:

Specific OIG Response:

We agree that the statements of facts in our report regarding risk assessment recommendations, guidance, and the data derived from the scientific literature are accurate. We differ on how to interpret and apply these facts to the characterization of the public health risk. Our report represents a creative and innovative application of these facts to the risk assessment to improve the risk assessment process by reducing the amount of uncertainty. Our intention with the report is to challenge the use of the status quo single chemical risk assessment approach initially developed by the FDA 56 years ago and subsequently adopted by EPA.

In our opinion, the risk assessment community has been slow to act on recommendations to improve the risk assessment process. Environmental risk assessments can be improved by reducing the sources of uncertainties in the process. Our report addresses 11 sources of uncertainty and implements four NAS recommendations to improve the risk assessment. By contrast, the current single chemical risk assessment process used by EPA addresses uncertainty by the subjective application of UFs whose magnitude is determined by consensus opinion and cannot be independently confirmed through direct scientific measurement. EPA should thoroughly examine our cumulative risk assessment approach and evaluate how accurately it predicts adverse outcomes or endpoints in exposed populations.

1. The early parts of the document lay out those Agency science policy documents that argue in favor of cumulative risk assessment as a more realistic approach to estimating the status of an exposed population. While this approach is directionally correct, it is one that has only received limited application across the Agency because of the highly data intensive nature of the assessments.

OIG Response:

Section 2 of our report identifies multiple sources within the science community that state that the cumulative risk assessment approach represents a "more realistic" characterization of the risk to public health from environmental exposures. Your comment states your agreement with this, but indicates the Agency does not pursue cumulative risk assessments because of the highly data-intensive nature of the assessments (i.e., increased level of effort needed to accomplish them). Therefore, your comment implies the Agency continues to use and rely on the lower-quality single chemical risk assessments because they are cheaper and easier to accomplish.

We agree that the preferred cumulative assessment approach is frequently unachievable for most compounds because of the limited amount of scientific information on the mechanism of toxicity, the dose-response relationship, the pharmacokinetics, the chemical exposure levels observed in the population, the relative potencies of the chemicals, and the potential interaction between chemicals. The cumulative risk assessment approach is impractical for chemicals that act at multiple sites in the body, act through several mechanisms of toxicity, are metabolized into several reactive chemicals, do not lend themselves to establishing a dose-response curve at human exposure levels, and lack information on their relative potencies or interactions.

However, this is not the case with this public health issue. The NIS stressors are actually technically well suited for a cumulative risk assessment approach. They act at only one sight in the body and act principally through only one enzyme in the body. They are not extensively metabolized or stored in the body. Everyone in the human population is continuously exposed to all four NIS stressors. The NIS stress level that induces adverse effects in humans is known and is detectable and observed within a small subset of the human population. The relative potencies of the NIS stressors are known. The chemical interaction between the NIS stressors is known and is ideal for risk assessment purposes (i.e., they act as dilutions of one another). In our opinion, the NIS stressors represent a simplified case for the application of cumulative risk assessment. In other words, if the risk assessment community will not attempt to implement a cumulative risk assessment approach to this public health issue, then there is little reason to believe that the cumulative risk assessment approach can be successfully applied to any other set of chemicals, because their biological activity is surely more complex than the NIS stressors.

2. There appears to be a strong implication that lacking a cumulative risk assessment, incremental risk reduction by considering individual chemicals is not appropriate. This argument is not science-based and does not belong in this document. This discussion reflects interpretation of the Agency's public health goals and should be raised in some other venue.

OIG Response:

We identified multiple sources that characterized the single chemical risk assessment approach as being outdated (EPA 1992; NAS 1994; EPA 1997b; EPA 2000; Callahan 2007). Furthermore, in Section 2 of our report, we identified multiple recommendations to EPA from multiple sources on how to improve the risk assessment process. We merged these recommendations with the biological knowledge that the thyroid is exposed and must react to the combined stress from all four NIS stressors. A single chemical risk assessment evaluates an incomplete, unrealistic exposure scenario in which the other three NIS stressors act as confounding factors. In our opinion, this issue is science based and is directly germane to the accurate and complete characterization of the risk to public health. As such, the decision to utilize a single chemical risk assessment approach or a cumulative risk assessment approach is directly relevant to the complete and accurate characterization of this public health issue and does belong in our report.

In our opinion, regardless of the risk assessment approach utilized (i.e., single or cumulative), the Agency's public health goal remains the same. The public should be protected from the occurrence of adverse effects resulting from exposure to excessive NIS stress.

3. The use of *in vitro* data in support of risk assessment was endorsed as a step forward in the National Academy of Sciences (NAS) report *Toxicity Testing in the 21st Century*. However, that report also noted the very large amount of effort remaining in order to understand how and when to use *in vitro* data in lieu of whole animal or human data, commenting that the workgroup anticipated that the development process was likely to span two decades. The OIG report relies heavily on the relative affinities of anions with the sodium/iodide symporter (NIS) to develop relative potency factors (RPFs) for the anion cluster. While interesting, this approach fails to account for many other physiological factors that may impact toxicity at different life stages and among species.

OIG Response:

In our general overall response and our response to ORD's comments, we provide an extensive discussion on our use of *in vitro* data in our cumulative risk assessment.

In our general overall response and our response to ORD's comments, we provide an extensive discussion how our cumulative risk assessment addresses uncertainty in comparison to a single chemical risk assessment.

4. The report discusses the uncertainties underlying the NAS reference dose (RfD) for perchlorate. It then proceeds to lay out the development of an RfD for NIS that contains many counter-conservative assumptions and nonstandard selections of endpoints and uncertainty factors for three compounds. This process is further complicated by the overlay of the RPFs.

OIG Response:

This is not a comment that addresses a specific scientific issue, but identifies some differences observed in our cumulative risk assessment that are not typical of a standard single chemical risk assessment approach.

This comment expresses confusion on the part of OW staff in what is technically presented in our cumulative risk assessment. EPA identifies in *EPA's Strategic Plan for Evaluating the Toxicity of Chemicals* that it "lacks the appropriate expertise" to implement the NAS Committee's vision and strategy for toxicity testing in the 21st century (EPA 2009, p 6). EPA further states that "additional training of existing staff and hiring staff conversant in the state-of-the-science knowledge in fields such as toxicology, biochemistry, bioformatics, etc" (EPA 2009, p 6). This comment provides an example of EPA's lack of appropriate expertise. Our cumulative risk assessment executes the NAS Committee's vision and strategy for toxicity testing.

The comment also contains incorrect information. Our report did not apply UFs for three compounds. The selection and magnitude of uncertainty factors is the principal task in a single chemical risk assessment. This conventional risk assessment mindset among EPA staff is carried over to the evaluation of our cumulative risk assessment. In Section 9.4.3, our cumulative risk assessment applies only a single UF of 1.5 to the %TIU$_{(NOAEL)}$ to derive the proposed %TIU$_{(RfD)}$. The %TIU is a measure of the total NIS stress level acting on the thyroid from the combined effect from exposure to all four NIS stressors. The UF was applied to the integrated effect of all the NIS stressors and not to each of the individual NIS stressors. Furthermore, the size of our 1.5 UF is unconventional but necessary because the thyroid's dose-response curve to NIS stress is U-shaped (i.e., either too much or too little NIS stress induces adverse effects). This complicity in our cumulative risk assessment is necessary and is driven by the nature of the problem being characterized (i.e., because the thyroid is exposed to multiple NIS stressors and its response is a nontypical, U-shaped, dose-response curve).

This comment also expresses that our use of relative potency factors (RPFs) "further complicate[s]" the risk assessment. The use of RPFs is a fundamental tool in risk assessment that is used to combine the exposures of multiple chemicals that act through the same mechanism and induce the same effect. Since the thyroid is known to be exposed to multiple NIS stressors, the use of RPFs is both necessary and appropriate. For OW to criticize our use of RPFs because they "complicate" our risk assessment is uninformed and demonstrates a lack of expertise in the use and application of other risk assessment techniques other than the standard single chemical risk assessment.

5. The review of exposure to various subpopulations and life stages is nicely done. Unfortunately, this section once again appears to focus on making the argument that incremental risk reduction is not appropriate, or put another way, EPA should approach regulation of adverse effects on an "all or nothing" basis.

OIG Response:

Identifying the exposure to the NIS stressors in various subpopulations and life stages is essential to fully characterize the risk to the public. As such, our report specifically identifies the exposure to the NIS stressors in various subpopulations and life stages.

We disagree with the characterization of incremental risk. A single chemical risk assessment identifies an acceptable exposure level (i.e., the RfD). This is equivalent to the "all or nothing" analogy in the comment. In other words, exposure below the RfD is expected to be without adverse effects while exposure above the RfD risks the occurrence of adverse effects. The single chemical risk assessment approach is neither designed nor attempts to measure, quantify, or identify incremental increases in risk with corresponding increases in exposure.

By contrast, our cumulative risk assessment provides substantially more detail on the characterization of this public health issue. Our cumulative risk assessment identifies the NIS stress level corresponding to the RfD, NOAEL, and LOAEL. The NIS stress level is the combined biological effect acting on the thyroid from the exposure to all four NIS stressors. The NIS stress level is measured as %TIU. As the NIS stress level increases during pregnancy (i.e., at lower %TIU levels), the frequency of occurrence of adverse effects and the observed severity of the adverse effect (e.g., cognitive deficit) increases in the offspring. The public health issue does not exhibit an exposure level that results in an "all or nothing" occurrence of adverse effects. In other words, the lower the %TIU level, the greater the risk for the occurrence and severity of adverse effects.

However, our cumulative risk assessment does characterize the change in the NIS stress level (i.e., %TIU) resulting from incremental changes in exposure to one or more of the individual NIS stressors. Understanding the contribution to risk from each of the NIS stressors is critical to fully characterize and effectively manage this public health issue. Further limiting the exposure to the NIS stressor that contributes the least amount of stress on the thyroid is neither an effective nor efficient public health strategy to decrease the ongoing occurrence of cognitive effects in children born to mothers in the United States currently exposed to excessive NIS stress levels during pregnancy and lactation.

6. A large portion of the risk characterization focuses on the status of iodide nutrition in the US and its impact on thyroid hormone status. This factor is beyond the purview of EPA regulatory activities. While potentially important, the Agency has no statutory basis to impact it. As such, it is simply the background against which an EPA risk assessment is developed and a constant for all intents and purposes.

OIG Response:

In our report, iodide nutrition becomes a prominent aspect of our cumulative risk assessment because it is the key to being able to understand and fully characterize this public health issue. Although our report considers and characterizes the contribution that all four NIS stressors have on this public health issue, iodide nutrition becomes prominent in the analysis because the lack of iodide stressor contributes the largest amount of risk to this public health issue. Furthermore, the exposure to the lack of iodide stressor is sufficiently large in a small portion of the U.S. population to detect and identify adverse effects from exposure during pregnancy and lactation. Since the lack of iodide stressor induces adverse effects in humans, this fact allows our analysis to identify a LOAEL and NOAEL to excessive exposure to NIS stress using the same technique applied during a single chemical risk assessment.

This OW comment is not consistent with previous EPA actions regarding the consideration dietary iodide has on this public health issue. Specifically, in 2003, EPA charged the NAS Committee to "consider the influence of iodide in the diet on the [perchlorate exposure] levels at which adverse effects would be observed" (NAS 2005, p 30). Clearly, in 2003, EPA believed that dietary iodide played a role in body's ability to tolerate NIS inhibition. For OW to argue now against the consideration of the role that dietary iodide has on this public health issue is unsupported.

This comment implies federal agencies can only consider and characterize that portion of the problem that fits within their statutory authority. If this limitation were followed, the federal government would be unable to fully consider any complex problem that spans more than one regulatory authority. We believe this type of restrictive management philosophy builds artificial walls between agencies and organizations that hinder or prevent the government from acting as a whole to effectively address a complex problem. Further, this restriction does not hold true for EPA on other issues. EPA routinely works with other federal, state, and local agencies to address complex problems spanning multiple regulatory authorities. The following are a few examples of multiagency efforts to address complex problems:

- EPA works with the U.S. Department of Agriculture (USDA) to address environmental contamination from pesticide and fertilizer runoff.

- EPA works with USDA and FDA to address pesticide residues in food.

- EPA works with the U.S. Department of Energy (DOE) and the Nuclear Regulatory Commission (NRC) work together to oversee the safe operation of nuclear power plants and their disposal of spent radioactive waste.

- EPA works with the U.S. Department of Transportation (DOT) to decrease vehicle emissions by increasing fuel economy standards.

We do agree with the comment that EPA does not have the statutory authority to act on insufficient dietary iodide levels in the population during pregnancy and lactation. Therefore, to address this public health issue, EPA would have to work with FDA and the Institute of Medicine (IOM) to evaluate and consider implementing iodide supplementation during pregnancy and lactation.

We **strongly disagree** with the recommendation to consider dietary iodide as "background" and to treat dietary iodide as a "constant for all intents and purposes" in this risk assessment. We disagree with this recommendation for the following reasons:

- OW's proposed assumption that dietary iodide intake in the U.S. population is a constant does not agree with the known NHANES survey data and is, therefore, unrealistic. The NHANES III survey identified that the iodide UIC at the 5th to the 95th percentile in the U.S. population ranged from 30 μg/L to 1134 μg/L (NAP 2000, pp 690-91, table G-6). This range is over an order of magnitude. In other words, within the middle 90% of the U.S. population, individual dietary iodide intakes vary by a factor of 37.8 times. Clearly, iodide intake is not a constant in the U.S. population.

- OW's recommendation to treat dietary iodide as a constant demonstrates a lack of understanding of the potential for confounding variables during a single chemical risk assessment. A confounding factor can severely skew the findings of a single chemical risk assessment when the confounding factor has a stronger effect than the chemical being studied and when the exposure to the confounding factor varies within the population.

- OW's recommendation goes against the basic biological premise of this public health issue, which is to ensure an adequate supply of iodide to the thyroid, to allow for the proper production and supply of thyroid hormone to the body in order to maintain public health. Under the mild goitrogen loads observed in the U.S. population, if the diet does not supply the body with enough iodide, no amount of NIS inhibitor reduction can compensate for an inadequate supply of iodide in the diet. This relationship and approach is observed in the medical treatment of endemic cretinism, where elevated goitrogen loads occur. The treatment is to increase iodide intake (not to lower the goitrogen load) to avoid adverse effects from an inadequate iodide uptake by the thyroid.

7. The report appears to propose iodide supplementation as a means for addressing the effects of goitrogens at large. However, no discussion of the potential toxicity of excess iodide is provided. Toxicity could occur in that portion of the population that is currently receiving sufficient iodide if exposure were significantly increased. Iodide has a classic U-shaped dose-response curve that is often seen for nutrients, expressing toxicity both at low and high concentrations, but having beneficial effects at mid-range doses. Supplementation would be particularly problematic for young children who are currently estimated to receive adequate iodide in their diet and who are highly susceptible to the effects of excess iodide.

OIG Response:

This comment mischaracterizes the content of our report. This type of mischaracterization is detrimental to the process of characterizing and addressing this public health issue. These include the following items:

- Our report **does not** recommend iodide supplementation to the entire public at large. Section 10.2.1.1.1 of our report is titled "Iodide Supplementation during Pregnancy and Lactation." Our conclusion is to propose iodide supplementation only for the subpopulation that is pregnant or lactating. Part of this subpopulation in the United States is being exposed to an excessive NIS stress level that leads to permanent cognitive deficits. Any iodide supplementation during pregnancy and lactation should occur as a regular part of prenatal care.

- Our report correctly identifies the potential for toxicity from an excess intake of iodide. In Section 9.4.2 and 10.2.1.1, we identify that an excess iodide intake occurs in pregnant women when the UIC exceeds 500 ug/L (ATA 2006). Furthermore, our report identifies that a UIC of 500 ug/L corresponds to an excess %TIU limit of 245% in pregnant women.

- Our report correctly identifies the dose-response curve for iodide as being U shaped. In Section 10.2.1.1.1, we state, "The risk from iodide intake is U-shaped". In Section 9.4.2, we identify the bounds of the U-shape iodide dose-response curve as being from a UIC of 50 ug/L (i.e., lower limit) to 500 ug/L (i.e., upper limit). Furthermore, we identify that a UIC of 50 μg/L and 500 μg/L result in a %TIU in a pregnant woman of 24.5 %TIU$_{(LOAEL)}$ and 245 %TIU$_{(excess\ limit)}$, respectively.

- The OW statement regarding iodide supplementation of young children is incorrect. Our report **does not** recommend iodide supplementation of young children. In Section 8.3, we identify through the FDA Total Dietary Study that young children are getting an adequate intake of iodide.

OW's comments included repetitive mischaracterization of the content of our report, which brings into question the thoroughness of their review. Since the potential regulation of perchlorate is a critical environmental decision, we believe OW should have conducted a more substantial, critical review of the *OIG Scientific Analysis of Perchlorate (External Review Draft)*.

If you have any questions about our comments, you can contact me or Elizabeth Doyle, Chief of the Human Health Risk Assessment Branch in the Office of Science and Technology, at 202-566-0056.

cc: Kevin Teichman, ORD Deputy Assistant Administrator for Science

OIG Response to EPA's Office of Children's Health Protection and Environmental Education Comments

Note: On September 2, 2008, the OIG distributed to the Agency a discussion draft of our *OIG Scientific Analysis of Perchlorate* for review and comment. On September 22, 2008, the Office of Children's Health Protection and Environmental Education (OCHPEE) provided the following comments on our discussion draft. When the OIG requested to meet with OCHPEE to discuss its comments, OCHPEE refused to meet. After OCHPEE's review of our discussion draft, OCHPEE chose to no longer participate in the OIG's review of perchlorate. Therefore, OCHPEE did not provide comments on our December 30, 2008, external review draft. However, for completeness, the OIG has provided a copy of OCHPEE's comments to our discussion draft and is providing a response to them here.

Review of OIG Scientific Analysis of Perchlorate: Supplemental Report (Discussion Draft) Dated September 2, 2008

Review Dated September 22, 2008 by Michael Firestone, Ph.D., Science Director, OCHPEE, EPA

Based on my overview of not only the OIG risk assessment, but the ICF review of the OIG assessment, I have reached the following conclusions:

1. I am supportive of the concept of applying cumulative risk considerations to questions regarding the risk of perchlorate vis-à-vis exposure to other inhibitors of the Na^+-Iodide symporter (NIS) including thiocyanate and nitrate.

OIG Response:

> *OCHPEE supports the application of a cumulative risk assessment to this public health issue. However, OCHPEE qualifies its support to the consideration of only the NIS inhibitors (i.e., thiocyanate, nitrate, and perchlorate). OCHPEE excludes the inclusion of the lack of iodide stressor. To us, OCHPEE's support for using only three of the four NIS stressors in a cumulative risk assessment is neither apparent nor defensible on procedural or scientific grounds. OCHPEE does not provide an explanation or justification for its position on using only three of the four NIS stressors in a cumulative risk assessment. Since OCHPEE declined to meet with us after our issuance of the discussion draft on September 2, 2008, we were not able to clarify with OCHPEE why it supports using only three of the four NIS stressors in a cumulative risk assessment.*

2. That said, to better understand the problem, it would have been more informative to have been able to base the assessment on exposure data that simultaneously examined and directly linked exposure through diet and fluid intake in individuals to biomonitoring levels in the same individuals. Rather, OIG independently considered NHANES biomonitoring study summary results for iodide levels and intake estimates derived from

FDA's Total Diet Study to consider exposure through foods. Thus, directly linking iodide deficiency to exposure of all NIS inhibitors in specific individuals to food and fluid intake is not possible. Further, the NHANES data does not appear to reflect biomonitoring in young infants, a key lifestage.

OIG Response:

For our review, we would have appreciated knowing the identification of any available dataset that combines information on the dietary intake of the NIS stressors with concurrent information on their excretion (e.g., biomonitoring data). However, since OCHPEE declined to meet with us, we were not able to clarify with OCHPEE what information or dataset it wanted us to consider.

Our report uses both the NHANES data and FDA's Total Diet Study because they provide relevant data on the exposure levels to perchlorate and iodide. Furthermore, both are available in the public domain. Our analysis assumes that the exposure levels to each of the four NIS stressors can vary independently of one another. This is a reasonable assumption because numerous dietary sources exist for each of the NIS stressors and the consumption rate of each dietary source depends on individual dietary preferences. Contrary to the suggestion in the comment, our report does not link iodide deficiency with exposure to NIS inhibitors. Our report links adverse effects to specific NIS stress levels that can be generated by the excessive exposure to one or more of the NIS stressors. We would have liked to clarify this issue with OCHPEE. However, OCHPEE declined to meet with us to discuss this matter.

We agree that the NHANES III survey data do not provide biomonitoring data on children less than 6 years old, which includes life stage of young infants. However, this limitation in the NHANES dataset did not deter our effort to characterize the exposure to the NIS stressors in both nursing and non-nursing (i.e., bottle feed) infants.

3. OIG's risk assessment relies heavily on using the Tonacchera, et al (2004) paper to model competitive inhibition in humans – their study is based on data derived from a study exposing Chinese hamster ovary cells stably expressing human NIS. This study concluded that the "relative potency of ClO_4^- to inhibit $^{125}I^-$ uptake at the NIS was found to be 15, 30 and 240 times that of SCN^-, I^-, and NO_3^- respectively on a molar concentration basis, with no evidence of synergism, ... consistent with a common mode of action by these anions." However, as noted in the ICF review:

    > "... the *in vitro* model used by Tonacchera has a number of limitations that reduce its utility for quantitative risk assessment ... (in that their) model does not replicate important features of thyroid physiology that would affect maternal responses to thyroid stressors. ...In addition, it does not consider the complex and extensive network of controls in the hypothalamus-pituitary axis and liver ... In vitro measurements of NIS inhibition appear to be poor predictors of the key event in perchlorate neurodevelopmental toxicity, which is reduced maternal thyroxine levels during the first trimester of pregnancy."

OIG Response:

> *This quote from ICF International's technical review of our cumulative risk assessment should be considered in context. ICF's technical review developed its opinion on the toxicity of perchlorate solely from the findings of the CDC epidemiological studies. Due to the increased statistical power of the Blount analysis, ICF is comfortable with dismissing the findings from all other human perchlorate exposure studies. Therefore, ICF considers our cumulative risk assessment to be a "poor predictor" of perchlorate neurodevelopmental toxicity because it does not agree with the finding of the Blount analysis. Furthermore, ICF contends that no other human perchlorate study or analysis is a good predictor of perchlorate toxicity. However, the Blount analysis is unique and not observed or corroborated by any other dataset.*
>
> *We carefully considered ICF's opinion and rejected it. ICF's assertion that the increased statistical power of the Blount analysis outweighs all other scientific concerns and allows the risk assessor to dismiss the findings of all other perchlorate studies is not founded. In the evaluation of data, scientists can decide to include or exclude an outlying data point from a database. However, scientists cannot exclusively use only the outlying data point and discard the bulk of the dataset. ICF's recommendation to use the "outlying data point" (i.e., the Blount analysis) as the sole basis for deriving an exposure limit for a perchlorate risk assessment is not scientifically defensible and is inconsistent with the Agency's risk assessment policies, procedures, and guidance. A fundamental requirement for using a statistical model (or any model for that matter) in regulatory rulemaking is that the statistical model has to be independently corroborated using a different dataset and scientific technique. Our review finds that the Blount statistical model has not met the standard for corroboration set forth in this EPA guidance document.*

4. The draft OIG assessment is fundamentally incomplete in that it fails to adequately consider exposures and risk to young infants, a key concern expressed by EPA's Children's Health Protection Advisory Committee (March 8, 2006) → (http://yosemite.epa.gov/ochp/ochpweb.nsf/content/30806_3.htm/$file/30806_3.pdf). While the assessment does model NIS inhibition load, it fails to reach a conclusion about risk by simply declaring that "a cumulative risk assessment approach is needed ..." (p.85). I did note that the OIG draft does acknowledge that modeling for nursing infants "was not performed due to the lack of sufficient time ..."

OIG Response:

> *Sections 7.2.3 and 7.2.4 of our report consider the available information regarding the total NIS exposure to both nursing infants and non-nursing infants (i.e., bottle-fed babies), respectively. The fifth comment from OW regarding our report states, "The review of exposure to various subpopulations and life stages is nicely done." OW does*

not appear to concur with OCHPEE opinion in this area. We believe our report identifies and characterizes the risk to young infants within the limitations of the available data. However, OCHPEE states that our report is fundamentally incomplete because it fails to adequately consider the risk to young infants. Unfortunately, OCHPEE does not provide specific details in its comments on how our analysis is flawed in this area. Since OCHPEE declined to meet with us after our issuance of the discussion draft on September 2, 2008, we were not able to clarify with OCHPEE its concern with our analysis regarding the exposure risk in young infants.

At the time of the discussion draft, we believed we might be able to apply the in vitro *NIS Model of Competitive Inhibition to calculate a TIU value and %TIU value in nursing infants. A %TIU value was not calculated for nursing infants in the external review draft is because of a limitation of the available data. For the NIS Model to be able to calculate a TIU value or %TIU value in nursing infants, the NIS Model needs the blood serum concentration of each of the four NIS stressors from a population of nursing infants. From our review of the scientific literature, this information has not been collected or published (i.e., it is not available). Furthermore, this information cannot be estimated because pharmacokinetic models do not exist for thiocyanate, nitrate, or iodide. Therefore, our report is limited to evaluating the available information on the dietary intake of the NIS stressors in nursing and non-nursing infants.*

5. OIG identifies iodide deficiency as a an important stressor – however, the OIG risk assessment fails to consider that high maternal perchlorate levels have been associated with concurrent lowered iodide levels – thus, these two stressors may not be independent factors in leading to perchlorate risk.

OIG Response:

OCHPEE expresses concern that maternal exposures to high levels of perchlorate might lower iodide levels. Our analysis is aware of the concern that high maternal exposures to perchlorate might decrease the iodide content of breast milk. However, one of the principal scientists investigating this possibility concludes that "The real role, if any, of perchlorate in reduction of milk iodide levels is as yet unknown" (Kirk 2007, p 185).

In this comment, OCHPEE is concerned that high maternal perchlorate exposure might decrease iodide levels, thereby contributing to the "perchlorate risk." So OCHPEE is arguing here that our report should consider the potential perchlorate effect of lowing iodide levels because both contribute to the "perchlorate risk." However, in its first comment, OCHPEE states the lack of iodide should not be included in the risk assessment of this public health issue. In our opinion, OCHPEE should clarify its opinion on the role that iodide has on this public health issue. However, since OCHPEE declined to meet with us after our issuance of the discussion draft on September 2, 2008, we were not able to clarify this issue with OCHPEE.

6. Just because some stressors may exert a greater effect than others should not be taken as an excuse not to clean-up all problematic environmental contaminants. It seems very

unusual to recommend iodide supplementation as a fix for the cumulative problem related to both environmental contamination of perchlorate and nitrate and the public health issues associated with iodide deficiency. Rather, since fetal risk already occurs because many women are already iodide deficient, exposure to contaminants like perchlorate just increases the risk – I don't believe this should be an excuse to dismiss the problem of environmental contamination.

OIG Response:

This comment mischaracterizes our recommendation to consider iodide supplementation during pregnancy and lactation as an "excuse." Our cumulative risk assessment evaluated the incremental risk that exposure to each of the NIS stressors contributes to the occurrence of adverse effects in humans. Our analysis identified that further limiting the public's exposure to perchlorate below the RfD of 0.0007 mg/kg-day has only a minimal effect on lowering the occurrence of adverse effects in humans. In other words, even if perchlorate exposure could be eliminated in the U.S. population, this amount of NIS stress reduction is ineffective at significantly lowering the occurrence of adverse effects in children born to mothers exposed to excessive NIS stress from iodide deficiency during pregnancy and lactation. Our recommendation to consider iodide supplementation during pregnancy and lactation is not an excuse, but is the only viable remedy that significantly lowers the occurrence of neurodevelopmental effects occurring in children born to mothers with an elevated NIS stress level from iodide deficiency during pregnancy and lactation.

The comment also mischaracterizes our recommendation to consider iodide supplementation during pregnancy and lactation as a "fix" for environmental contamination. Apparently, OCHPEE does not understand the incremental risk that exposure to each of the individual NIS stressors contributes to this public health issue. This OCHPEE comment accepts the occurrence of neurodevelopmental effects to children born to mothers with iodide deficiency, but recommends action to lower the risk from environmental perchlorate exposure even though both perchlorate and lack of iodide act through the same biological mechanism of toxicity. For this public health issue, the distinction between attributing adverse effects induced from environmental contamination or iodide deficiency is artificial. Addressing only perchlorate contamination, as suggested, does not address the problem and we find this unacceptable.

OIG Response to Consolidated Comments from the Department of Defense

We find the consolidated comments from DOD to be generally supportive of our approach. In DOD's executive summary, it concludes that "[Our] approach is logical and incorporates the most recent risk assessment tools, advancements and recommendations." DOD states that its "technical comments are provided with the intent of bolstering the scientific credibility." We concur with the concept that science is a dynamic process in which the quality of the science is improved by the development and implementation of incremental steps. Our review finds that the implementation of a cumulative risk assessment approach is a critical step that must be taken by the risk assessment community to improve the characterization of the risks contributing to this public health issue. Although we would like to use DOD's comments to further develop, refine, and corroborate our cumulative risk assessment approach, our primary mission is not to conduct environmental risk assessments. We conducted this cumulative risk assessment to demonstrate, by example, how the numerous recommendations on how to improve environmental risk assessments could actually be implemented. We believe EPA needs leadership and a cultural paradigm shift within its risk assessment community to recognize the need for and benefits of moving beyond the status quo single chemical risk assessment approach to assessing risk that has been used for the last 56 years.

In lieu of responding to DOD individual comments, we refer DOD to our detailed explanation under our General Overall Response.

The consolidated comments from DOD on our external review draft are provided in their entirety in Appendix D.

OIG Response to Pirkle, Osterloh, and Blount Comments

 **DEPARTMENT OF HEALTH & HUMAN SERVICES**

Public Health Service

Centers for Disease Control
and Prevention (CDC)
Atlanta GA 30341-3724
February 4, 2009

Bill Roderick
Deputy Inspector General
c/o: OCPM (Mail code - 2491T) Room 3106
1200 Pennsylvania Avenue, NW
Washington, DC 20460

Re: Perchlorate Comments for the Office of
Inspector General (OIG)

Dear Mr. Roderick:

Please find attached scientific comments on the *OIG Scientific Analysis of Perchlorate (External Review Draft)*. These comments are the scientific opinions of the undersigned and do not necessarily represent the views of the Centers for Disease Control and Prevention.

Thank you for the opportunity to comment on this document.

Sincerely,

James L. Pirkle, M.D., Ph.D.
Deputy Director for Science
Division of Laboratory Sciences

Sincerely,

John D. Osterloh, M.D.
Chief Medical Officer
Division of Laboratory Sciences

Sincerely,

Benjamin C. Blount, Ph.D.
Chief, VOC and Perchlorate Laboratory
Division of Laboratory Sciences

Comments on "*OIG Scientific Analysis of Perchlorate (External Review Draft)*"

We feel that some statements found in Appendix A of the "*OIG Scientific Analysis of Perchlorate (External Review Draft)*" warrant comment. Specifically, the findings of Blount et al (2006) and Steinmaus et al (2007) *are* biologically coherent and focused on a large population with additional potential stressors of iodide uptake. The data set studied by Blount et al and Steinmaus et al is the *only set of data* that identifies a susceptible group (women with lower iodide concentrations) and measures (and adjusts for effects of) the other competing goitrogenic anions. That a population with lower iodide excretion showed a more pronounced association between thyroid hormone levels and perchlorate levels is coherent with the known mechanisms of the interactions of iodide and perchlorate. While the Blount analysis indicates a potential effect of perchlorate at levels below those seen in the Greer study, the OIG analysis suggests that some new mechanism should be postulated to account for this difference. A new mechanism is not required; only to examine the differences between the Greer study and the study analyzed by Blount et al and Steinmaus et al. The Greer study did not examine a susceptible population (women with lower iodide excretion), was not sufficiently powered to see small changes, and did not examine subjects under chronic exposure conditions or for an extended period of time after their experimental perchlorate exposure. It is therefore not surprising that the Greer study did not observe changes in thyroid function and the analyses by Blount et al and Steinmaus et al were able to detect these changes. It is also possible that mechanisms in addition to NIS inhibition are at play -- McClanahan et al (2009) recently published evidence that perchlorate can act via a second mechanism to impair thyroid hormone production/secretion.

In general, we are puzzled by the "critical review" of Blount et al and Steinmaus et al; this text is appended to the main body of the report, which lacks similar critical reviews of other recent publications on this topic. The authors of *Appendix A* state that "…repeating the analysis in the next NHANES data set would not represent an independent evaluation…" because the cross-sectional study design is the same as the study design used by Blount et al and Steinmaus et al. Yet the authors of *Appendix A* cite numerous conference abstracts that describe studies of much smaller populations, each utilizing a similar cross-sectional study design. The fact that similar cross-sectional designs are used in these studies is not cited as a lack of independent information. In our opinion, detailed study of perchlorate exposure and thyroid function in ~4000 new U.S. residents from a different NHANES study would provide additional valuable insight in a completely new population of individuals, and would provide additional important evidence concerning the relationship between thyroid function and perchlorate levels at the relatively low levels experienced by the general population.

In addition, the NHANES sample size is huge compared to the aggregate sum of persons in all these cross-sectional studies combined. The statistical power afforded by the large NHANES population size merits special consideration in light of the need for considerable statistical power to detect the effect sizes presented in the Blount et al and Steinmaus et al analyses.

Finally, the Blount analysis did not state or show that "13 µg/day of perchlorate exposure induces toxicity." This citation should be corrected.

Reference citations provided with CDC's comments are not repeated here but are available in Appendix D.

Specific OIG Response:

Our report conducted a critical review of CDC's epidemiological analysis because the finding from the Blount analysis (Blount 2006b) is often cited as the justification for a strict perchlorate drinking water limit. The technical review by ICF International recommends using the Blount analysis to justify a 6 ug/L drinking water limit. At the April 25, 2007, hearing before the House Subcommittee on Environment and Hazardous Materials titled "Perchlorate: Health and Environmental Impacts of Unregulated Exposure," the Blount analysis was a major topic of discussion. Likewise, at the May 6, 2008, hearing before the Senate Committee on Environment and Public Works titled "Perchlorate and TCE in the Nations Waters," the chairwoman cited the Blount analysis in her opening statement. Furthermore, CDC's epidemiological analysis is specifically cited in the comments from the EPA ORD. Since the Blount analysis suggests that the perchlorate toxicity is significantly more toxic (i.e., more than 300 times more toxic) than what the NAS Committee and all previous perchlorate studies have indicated, it would be inappropriate of us not to conduct a critical review of it. In his prepared statement at the congressional hearing before the House Subcommittee on the April 25, 2007, Dr. Pirkle stated the finding from the Blount analysis is "unexpected based on previous research" (House 2007, p 28).

In regard to the commenter's article claiming a second perchlorate toxicity mechanism that impairs thyroid hormone production and secretion, we reviewed the McLanahan rat study (McLanahan 2009). The NAS Committee has already stated that the rat animal model is not well suited for evaluating the perchlorate toxicity in humans. Specifically, the NAS Committee states that rats are more sensitive to the effects of NIS stress (NAS 2005, pp 168–69). Therefore, the rat studies are inappropriate for determining the dose-response relationship in humans (NAS 2005, pp 168–69). Therefore, any proposed mechanism of toxicity reported in a rat model is not particularly meaningful from a human health risk perspective until that mechanism of toxicity is also observed and confirmed in human data. Based on NAS Committee's opinion on perchlorate rat studies, we find the continued study of perchlorate toxicity in rat data to be wasteful of resources when those same resources could better be used researching the observed toxicity in humans from excessive NIS stress during pregnancy and lactation.

We understand the scientific concept that as the size of an epidemiological study increases, so does its statistical power. However, we reject the assertion by both CDC and ICF International that this benefit outweighs all other scientific concerns and allows the risk assessor to discard the findings of all other perchlorate studies. Our review identified that the findings from the Blount analysis did not meet the Agency's requirements for use as the basis for environmental rulemaking. For example, since the Blount analysis is a statistical model, it needs to meet the standards set forth in EPA's 2003 *Draft Guidance on the Development, Evaluation, and Application of Regulatory Environmental Models* (EPA 2003a) before legitimately being used for environmental rulemaking. A principal standard is that all statistical models must be corroborated. Our review finds that the Blount statistical model has not met the standard for corroboration set forth in this EPA guidance. Furthermore, we have provided an extensive explanation of our assessment of the CDC's epidemiological studies in Appendix A, our workpaper documenting our meeting with ICF International on their technical review (available in Appendix D), and in our responses to the comments from both EPA's ORD and MassDEP.

We also have a concern that the CDC epidemiological studies did not adequately consider homeostasis. Specifically, the findings from the CDC epidemiological studies argue against thyroid homeostasis. The Blount analysis reports that a small increase in the thyroid's NIS stress level in women with a UIC of <100 ug/L results in a change in serum T_4 levels (Blount 2006b, table 6). However, the hypothalamus-pituitary-thyroid (HPT) axis is a biological feedback mechanism that compensates for changes in the body's NIS stress level to maintain an adequate supply of thyroid hormones for proper health. Therefore, the classical dose-response curve is not expected to be observed (i.e., a change in the dose results in a change in the response). Within the NIS stress levels that the HPT axis has the ability to compensate for, the observed thyroid hormones levels in the blood should remain constant. In other words, given enough time for the HPT axis to compensate, an increase in NIS stress at the lower levels of stress would be expected to result in no change in the thyroid hormones levels in the blood. However, at NIS stress levels above the HPT axis's ability to compensate (i.e., thyroid at the maximum hormone-producing efficiency), an additional increase in NIS stress would be expected to result in a corresponding decrease in the thyroid hormones levels in the blood. Therefore, in response to increasing NIS stress levels, the thyroid's hormone production should be bimodal (i.e., the response should be flat within the HPT axis's ability to compensate and should decrease once the HPT axis's ability to compensate is exhausted). This expected bimodal response of the thyroid is not observed in CDC epidemiological studies.

When considering the effect that homeostasis has on thyroid performance, the CDC epidemiological studies are attempting to detect an adverse thyroid effect when the vast majority of individuals in the NHANES dataset are not exposed to excessive NIS stress levels. The NAS Committee states, "Hypothyroidism occurs only if daily iodide intake is below about 10 to 20 µg" (NAS 2005, p 6). An intake of only 10 to 20 µg of iodide equates to severe iodide deficiency. Using the distribution in the NHANES III survey as an example, at the 5th percentile, all age groups are above this level. However, about 10% of the pregnant and/or lactating subpopulation in the NHANES III survey has UIC levels at or below < 50 ug/L, which represents an excessive NIS stress level for this life stage that potentially leads to the occurrence of hypothyroxinemia. Of the 21,298 individuals in the NHANES III survey, only 871 are pregnant and/or lactating, of which only about 10% are exposed to excessive NIS stress levels (i.e., about 87 pregnant and/or lactating women). Therefore, only about 87 of the 21,298 individuals (i.e., 0.4%) in the NHANES III survey are exposed to an excessive NIS stress level that would be expected to generate abnormal thyroid hormone levels. Therefore, the statistical advantage of using the NHANES dataset is lost in the CDC epidemiological studies when the vast majority of the individuals within the NHANES datasets have not exhausted their HPT axis's ability to compensate for their NIS stress level.

At the end of its comments, CDC requests that the OIG correct our statement that the Blount analysis shows that "13 ug/day of perchlorate exposure induces toxicity." We agree that the Blount paper does not make the specific statement that "13 ug/day of perchlorate exposure induces toxicity." However, a common interpretation of the Blount analysis is that the observed perchlorate toxicity justifies implementing a strict perchlorate drinking water limit. For example, the technical review by ICF International argues that the Blount analysis justifies setting the perchlorate drinking water limit at 6 ppb (i.e., the 13 ug/day represents the LOAEL subsequently divided by 2 liters/day drinking water consumption with no application of uncertainty factors gives a perchlorate drinking water limit of 6.5 ppb (rounded to 6 ppb)). (Note: The OIG does not agree with ICF International's assessment of the Blount analysis.) Therefore, since the common interpretation of the Blount analysis is that perchlorate is inducing toxicity at 13 ug/day, we will keep this language in our report. However, if the CDC believes that the Blount analysis does not show perchlorate toxicity, we encourage the CDC to interpret and publish the scientific meaning of their own study to correct the apparent widespread misinterpretation and use of its finding among the risk assessment community.

OIG Response to Alabama Department of Environmental Management's Comments

ONIS "TREY" GLENN, III
DIRECTOR

ADEM

Alabama Department of Environmental Management
adem.alabama.gov
1400 Coliseum Blvd. 36110-2059 ♦ Post Office Box 301463
Montgomery, Alabama 36130-1463
(334) 271-7700
FAX (334) 271-7950

BOB RILEY
GOVERNOR

March 9, 2009

Attn: Perchlorate Comments for the OIG
c/o: OCPM (Mail code - 2491T) Room 3106
1200 Pennsylvania Avenue, NW
Washington, DC 20460

Re: **ADEM Review Comments:** *EPA Office of Inspector General Scientific Analysis of Perchlorate (External Review Draft)*, dated December 30, 2008.

Dear Sir or Madam:

The Alabama Department of Environmental Management (ADEM or the Department) has completed its review of the referenced *Office of Inspector General (OIG) Scientific Analysis of Perchlorate.* This document is being distributed to receive scientific comments on the use and application of a cumulative risk assessment approach to characterizing the public health risk from a low Total Iodine Uptake during pregnancy and lactation. ADEM has generated the enclosed comments.

If you have any questions regarding this correspondence, please contact Sarah Gill at (334) 271-7734 or via e-mail at sgill@adem.state.al.us or Mr. Prem Kumar at (334) 394-4377 or via e-mail at KPKumar@adem.state.al.us.

Sincerely,

Wm. Gerald Hardy, Chief
Land Division

Enclosure

Birmingham Branch
110 Vulcan Road
Birmingham, AL 35209-4702
(205) 942-6168
(205) 941-1603 (Fax)

Decatur Branch
2715 Sandlin Road, S. W.
Decatur, AL 35603-1333
(256) 353-1713
(256) 340-9359 (Fax)

Mobile Branch
2204 Perimeter Road
Mobile, AL 36615-1131
(251) 450-3400
(251) 479-2593 (Fax)

Mobile - Coastal
4171 Commanders Drive
Mobile, AL 36615-1421
(251) 432-6533
(251) 432-6598 (Fax)

ADEM Review Comments:
Office of Inspector General Scientific Analysis of Perchlorate
Dated December 30, 2008

<u>Reviewer 1 Comments:</u>

1. **Page 141, Section 9.1.4 Perchlorate PBPK and the Greer Perchlorate Exposure Study:** The paper states "*The %TIUs calculated from the Tonacchera Model for an external perchlorate dose for 0.007 and 0.5 mg/kg-day are in excellent agreement with the %TIU observed in the Greer study (see table above). However, the %TIUs calculated from the Tonacchera Model for an external perchlorate dose for 0.02 and 0.1 mg/kg-day are not in particularly good agreement with the %TIU observed in the Greer study (see table above). In short, half of the %TIU values results agree, while the other half of %TIU values do not agree so well.*" This appears to be the extent of the data analysis comparing the observed and predicted data. The author(s) should consider plotting the data and performing a regression analysis or some other form of statistical analysis. A simple linear regression, comparing the observed %TIU in the Greer study to the %TIU predicted by the Tonacchera model for the same perclorate dose, yields an R^2 of 0.92, a slope of 0.99, and an intercept of 6.14. These results indicate a high degree of agreement between the predicted and observed data. Given the limited number of data points (four) available for comparison, no definitive conclusion can be made that the model accurately predicts the %TIU at a given perchlorate dose, but, by the same token, no definitive conclusion can be made that the model does not accurately predict the %TIU at a given perchlorate dose.

Specific OIG Response:

We chose to evaluate the Tonacchera Model against the Greer study at each external perchlorate dose to highlight that the Greer study design does not attempt to control for confounding values. The Greer study design does not measure for the exposure to the other three known NIS stressors (i.e., lack of iodide, thiocyanate, and nitrate). Therefore, the exposures to the other three NIS stressors act as confounding variables in the Greer study. This introduces considerable variability into the actual level of NIS stress acting on the thyroid at each dose. As such, excellent agreement is not expected when the Tonacchera Model, which considers the total NIS stress level, is compared to the Greer dataset, which measures the exposure to only one NIS stressor.

2. **Page 174, Section 9.1 Corroboration of Tonacchera Model with Effects Observed in Humans:** The final sentence in this section states "*Since a pinch of table salt weighs about 460 mg, 14.3 mg of salt is equivalent to about 1/32nd of a pinch of salt. Since a smidgen of table salt weighs about 230 mg, 14.3 mg of salt is equivalent to about 1/16th a smidgen of salt.*" There is no scientifically accepted standard measurement for a 'pinch' and a 'smidgen'. Therefore, it is suggested that the above statement be removed from page 174 and page 184.

Specific OIG Response:

Although not used as scientific measurements, a 'pinch' and 'smidgen' are measurements used in cooking. Since one of the NIS stressors is a dietary nutrient, we believe the use of cooking terms for measurements is appropriate. These terms were used to identify in practical cooking terms how much intake of iodized salt would be needed to offset a 1.0% reduction in %TIU in pregnant women that is estimated to occur when drinking water exposure to perchlorate increases from 6.1 ppb to 24.5 ppb. This comparison identifies the small amount of NIS stress that is induced by the consumption of drinking water containing perchlorate at 24.5 ppb and how small of an amount of iodized salt is needed to offset this NIS stress level.

3. **Page 190, Appendix A:** The test states *"The R^2 value of 0.240 reported in the Blount analysis shows that perchlorate accounts for only 3% of the variation seen in the serum tT4 (Charnely 2008)."* The R^2 value is the proportion of variability in a data set that is accounted for by the statistical model and ranges from 0 to 1. If R^2 is 0.24, then 24%, not 3%, of the variation is predicted by the Blount analysis. Also, the reference quoted is not included in the list of references in Appendix B.

Specific OIG Response:

The R^2 value of 0.240 signifies that all the terms in the statistical model used in the Blount analysis account for 24% of the variation observed in the NHANES dataset. However, perchlorate is only one of several terms in the statistical model. Dr. Charnely is reporting that the single perchlorate term in the statistical model account for only 3% of the variation.

The Charnely 2008 citation was accidently omitted in the references. This error has been corrected in the final.

4. While the paper is titled "Scientific Analysis of Perchlorate", it is actually an analysis of the use of cumulative risk assessment to evaluate NIS inhibition. The author(s) provide a good summary of past studies on NIS inhibition and present several valid points regarding the relative impacts of iodide nutritional deficiency, nitrate, thiocyanate, and perchlorate on the thyroid. However, there are still uncertainties and obstacles to applying a cumulative risk assessment (see Reviewer 2's comments) that are not acknowledged in the paper.

Specific OIG Response:

Our title reflects our science review of the Agency's risk assessment policies, procedures, guidance, and recommendations and our analysis of their implementation by the Agency to effectively evaluate the risk from perchlorate. Our analysis concludes that a cumulative risk assessment approach is required to improve the characterization of the risk. To demonstrate this point, we conducted and provided a cumulative risk assessment of this public health issue.

In our General Overall Response to the comments, we provide an extensive discussion and comparison of uncertainties between the single chemical risk assessment approach and the cumulative risk assessment approach to this public health issue.

5. The paper contains a large number of grammatical errors, which in a few places are significant enough to make it difficult to understand what the author(s) intended to convey. It is suggested that the author(s) have the paper edited to address grammatical errors.

Specific OIG Response:

OIG reports are edited prior to release; however, that does not mean that all errors are identified. We are satisfied that the errors were minor and trivial and have been addressed.

Sarah Gill, Ph.D., PE
Alabama Department of Environmental Management
1400 Coliseum Blvd
Montgomery, AL 36110-2059
Phone: 334-271-7734
E-Mail: sgill@adem.state.al.us
Background: Ph.D. Civil Engineering
Area of Expertise: Environmental engineering

Reviewer 2 Comments:

These comments are regarding the US Environmental Protection Agency Office of Inspector General (OIG) Scientific Analysis of Perchlorate (External Review Draft) report, which is being distributed to receive scientific comments on the use and application of a cumulative risk assessment approach to characterizing the public health risk from a low Total Iodine Uptake during pregnancy and lactation. A review of scientific literature was performed to derive these comments.

CUMULATIVE RISK ASSESSMENT APPROACH

The cumulative risk assessment approach using the dose addition method for all four sodium iodide symporter (NIS) stressors to characterize the risk to public health from a low total iodide uptake (TIU) during pregnancy and lactation is a very novel approach, but reviewing the literature pertaining to this area shows that very little quantitative data is available to support this approach, especially for pregnancy and lactation. Differential exposure to mixtures of environmental agents, especially chemical stressors, can contribute to increased vulnerability of human population. Cumulative Risk Assessment is a tool for organizing and analyzing information to evaluate the probability and seriousness to multiple environmental stressors, and is hampered by three interrelated problems:

1. Relatively little is known about magnitude, duration, frequency and timing of cumulative exposure to these important environmental mixtures.
2. Scant evidence is available on whether mixture-related effects are additive at exposure levels during pregnancy and lactation.
3. There is inadequate knowledge and insufficient understanding of the interactive mechanisms of toxicity that occur among mixture constituents.

Cumulative risk assessment will be most useful if the uncertainty factors/safety factors built into the conventional risk assessment process adequately protect the public health from cumulative effects within a sufficient margin of safety. A cumulative risk assessment approach as suggested by the OIG Analysis may provide guidance about which NIS inhibitors that are part of our day-to-day lives constitute a serious health risk that is not adequately accounted for by traditional risk assessment methods (Sexton and Hattis, 2007).

The application of a cumulative risk assessment approach to public health risk is in its infancy because of so many uncertainties. According to Dasgupta, *et al.* (2008), it may be doubtful that thiocyanate and/or nitrate pose a greater risk of low iodide uptake based on the selectivity factors for the NIS and projected dietary intake amounts with special reference to lactation (breastfed infants). Little nitrate is excreted in milk and bears little relationship to dietary nitrate.

Specific OIG Response:

> In our General Overall Response to the comments, we provide an extensive discussion and comparison of uncertainties between the single chemical risk assessment approach and the cumulative risk assessment approach to this public health issue.

For thiocyanate, neither urinary excretion nor ingested amounts may provide a reliable index of the circulating levels of thiocyanate seen by the mammary NIS. Urinary excretion may not reflect circulating levels because, in part, thiocyanate is formed *in vivo* from cyanide, is present in certain foods (Eminedoki, *et al.*, 1994), and is formed during protein metabolism (Himwich and Saunders, 1948). Cigarette smoke is an important source of hydrogen cyanide. The cyanide-to-thiocyanate conversion takes place in the liver and kidney. Ingested thiocyanate is known to be oxidized by a variety of mechanisms (Grisham and Ryan, 1990) and form various adducts (Funderburk and Van Middlesworth, 1967). Of interest is that thiocyanate also has benefits: its *lactoperoxidase*-mediated oxidation products are powerful protection against the human immunodeficiency virus (Wang, *et al.*, 2000).

Specific OIG Response:

> We concur with the fact that human exposure to both thiocyanate and nitrate is both exogenous and endogenous. Therefore, blood serum concentrations for both thiocyanate and nitrate cannot be determined from either the amount of ingestion or excretion. Therefore, to know the internal exposure of the thyroidal NIS and mammary NIS to thiocyanate and nitrate, direct blood sample measurements of thiocyanate and nitrate are needed in the study population. Our cumulative risk assessment understood this problem of determining the internal exposure levels of both thiocyanate and nitrate. During our analysis, we specifically searched for and utilized studies that measured the exposure levels of thiocyanate and/or nitrate in the blood (Banerjee 1997; Banerjee 1997b; Tajtáková 2006; Braverman 2005; Tellez 2005). Studies measuring the exposure levels of thiocyanate and/or nitrate in the blood are uncommon, but the identification of additional studies in the literature with this type of data would be valuable in the further validation and corroboration of the NIS Model.

There is no universal agreement on the extent of the threat posed by perchlorate during lactation (Braverman and Pearce, 2005; Kirk, *et al.*, 2005 and Lamm, *et al.*, 2005). There is no conclusive data as to if, and to what extent, perchlorate inhibits transport to human milk. Extrapolation from mouse NIS experiments to the human mother-infant pair is tenuous, especially when such *in vitro* experiments involve concentrations far removed from reality, and through the NIS in a manner different from that of iodide (Dohan, *et al.*, 2007).

According to Dasgupta, *et al.* (2008), until proven otherwise *in vivo*, the role of thiocyanate as an iodide transport inhibitor in human lactation, especially *vis-à-vis* perchlorate, should not be overemphasized, especially when such analysis is based on urinary thiocyanate content and selectivity factors determined *in vitro* on non-human NIS systems. They also opined that the impact of perchlorate and thiocyanate on inhibiting iodide transport in human milk (lactation) may have been overemphasized.

Specific OIG Response:

> We are aware of the concern that high maternal exposures to perchlorate might decrease the iodide content of breast milk. However, one of the principal scientists investigating this possibility concludes, "The real role, if any, of perchlorate in reduction of milk iodide levels is as yet unknown" (Kirk 2007, p 185).

> Our analysis is also aware that elevated maternal thiocyanate exposure might inhibit the transport of iodide by the mammary NIS and decrease the iodide content of breast milk. However, the primary source of elevated thiocyanate exposure in the United States is from smoking. Furthermore, smoking during pregnancy and lactation is already understood to adversely affect public health.

> In Section 7.2.3 of our report, we estimated the total goitrogen load acting on nursing infants by identifying studies that reported direct measurements of the concentration of thiocyanate and nitrate in the breast milk. Furthermore, we used the Clewell PBPK Model to estimate the perchlorate concentration in the breast milk from the mother's perchlorate exposure level. This analysis was done to better characterize the total goitrogen load acting on nursing infants. Our analysis shows that perchlorate exposure through breast milk at the RfD contributes up to 30% and 25% of the total goitrogen load at 1 month and 6 months, respectively.

Though OIG emphasizes the relevance of a cumulative risk approach using all the NIS stressors (perchlorate, thiocyanate, nitrate and the lack of iodide) to better characterize the risk to the public, according to Wilkinson, *et al.* (2000) it is important to emphasize that there remains a great deal of scientific uncertainty about how to proceed with cumulative risk assessment as described in the Food Quality Protection Act. The serious difficulties associated with defining common toxicity and "concurrent exposure", combined with the current paucity of data and methodology required to conduct cumulative risk assessment, suggest that the procedure is not yet ready for use in public health risk, especially to characterize TIU during pregnancy and lactation.

Specific OIG Response:

> In our General Overall Response to the comments, we provide an extensive discussion and comparison of uncertainties between the single chemical risk assessment approach and the cumulative risk assessment approach to this public health issue. We believe the cumulative risk assessment decreases the amount of uncertainty in the risk characterization of this public health issue.

In a single chemical risk assessment, the major task is to critique the quality of the chemical's toxicity dataset and apply UFs. This process is subjective and arbitrary. The NAS Committee identified that "no absolute rules exist for application of the [uncertainty] factors, and professional judgment is a large component of their use." (NAS 2005, p 29). The appropriateness of the amount of total UFs applied in a single chemical risk assessment cannot be independently confirmed or corroborated through direct scientific measurement.

By contrast, the scientific merit of our cumulative risk assessment can be directly evaluated by how accurately it predicts adverse and nonadverse effects. Given the exposure level to all four NIS stressors in a study population, the NIS Model can predict the amount of iodide uptake. This iodide uptake prediction can be compared against actual radioactive iodide uptake measurements taken in exposure studies such as the Greer study and the Braverman occupational study. Furthermore, given the exposure level to all four NIS stressors in a study population, the NIS Model can calculate a %TIU that can be compared against known NOAEL and LOAEL values to predict the type, severity, and occurrence of adverse effects for an adult male or female, pregnant woman, or fetus. Our cumulative risk assessment is an example of what the *EPA's Strategic Plan for Evaluating the Toxicity of Chemicals* calls a predictive risk assessment (EPA 2009, p 8).

Because of the complexity of considering so many factors simultaneously, there is a need for simplified risk assessment tools (such as software packages, databases and other modeling resources) that would allow screening level risk assessments and could allow communities and stakeholders to conduct risk assessment and thus increase stakeholder participation. In practice, measuring or estimating concurrent exposure to multiple stressors is not straightforward, even if the toxicologically relevant temporal and spatial aspects are known. There is no established state and federal environmental tracking system that provides systematic collection, integration, analysis, interpretation, and dissemination of information about the environmental hazards, including sources, environmental concentrations, exposures, doses, and potentially related health effects. The creation of linked monitoring systems, databases , and registries offers the prospect of better data on cumulative exposures and improved understanding of the connection between combined exposures and chronic health effects of thyroid inhibitors (Litt, *et al.*, 2004 and McGeehin, *et al.*, 2004).

Specific OIG Response:

Although we encourage the participation of communities and stakeholders in the preparation and evaluation of environmental risk assessments, the complexities and novelty of conducting a cumulative risk assessment is beyond the capabilities of simplified risk assessment tools (e.g., software packages, databases, and other modeling resources).

We agree that better human data are needed to improve the understanding and documentation of the chronic health effects from the concurrent exposure to all four NIS stressors. Epidemiological studies that evaluate the chronic exposure to NIS stress and the resulting health effects are needed. Since internal thiocyanate and nitrate exposure levels cannot be assessed through intake or excretion data, these epidemiological studies must determine exposure through the testing of blood samples.

Considering the lack of sufficient information about the effects of perchlorate in sensitive populations such as pregnant and lactating women, the recommendation of the National Academy of Sciences to define a no-observed-effect-level as a non-classic departure point for perchlorate risk assessment seems to be defensible. Looking at the mode of action and available scientific literature on the four NIS stressors on total iodine uptake during pregnancy and lactation, cumulative risk assessment is a holistic approach of combining the effects of exposure to multiple stressors via all relevant sources, pathways, and routes. The methods used in cumulative risk assessment are still being perfected and it is recommended that EPA and others continue research to make this approach more reliable, realistic and relevant. Since perchlorate has been determined to be the least of four stressors affecting iodine uptake and health effects to pregnant or lactating females, care should be taken by EPA not to rely heavily on limiting perchlorate exposure when effects from the other three stressors cannot be controlled.

Specific OIG Response:

Our analysis independently evaluated and confirmed that the NAS-recommended perchlorate RfD of 0.0007 mg/kg-day is conservative and protective of human health using a different risk assessment technique. However, the NAS Committee's use of a NOEL to derive the perchlorate RfD should not be used as a precedent to change EPA's risk management goal from preventing adverse effects in humans from environmental exposure to preventing all biological effects from occurring in humans from environmental exposure.

We agree that our cumulative risk assessment is a holistic approach. As more scientific information is learned, we encourage the risk assessment community to further develop, refine, and corroborate our cumulative risk assessment to make it more reliable, realistic, and relevant.

We agree with the commenter's assessment that EPA should not "rely heavily on limiting perchlorate exposure," but disagree with the concept that "the other three stressors can not be controlled." Our analysis indicates that iodide deficiency during pregnancy and lactation is a major concern and should be addressed.

K. Prem Kumar, Ph.D.
Alabama Department of Environmental Management
1400 Coliseum Blvd
Montgomery, AL 36110-2059
Phone: 334-394-4377
E-mail: KPKumar@adem.state.al.us
Background: M.P.H. Environmental Toxicology; Ph.D. Aquatic Biology
Area of Expertise: Environmental toxicology and environmental public health risk
    assessment

References citations provided with Alabama Department of Environmental Management's Comments are not repeated here but are available in Appendix D.

OIG Response to Massachusetts Department of Environmental Protection's Comments

COMMONWEALTH OF MASSACHUSETTS
EXECUTIVE OFFICE OF ENERGY & ENVIRONMENTAL AFFAIRS
DEPARTMENT OF ENVIRONMENTAL PROTECTION
ONE WINTER STREET, BOSTON, MA 02108 617-292-5500

DEVAL L. PATRICK
Governor

TIMOTHY P. MURRAY
Lieutenant Governor

IAN A. BOWLES
Secretary

LAURIE BURT
Commissioner

March 9, 2009

Office of the Inspector General
United State Environmental Protection Agency
Washington, D.C. 20460
Perchlorate_comments_for_OIG@EPA.gov

Dear Inspector General:

We are submitting the following comments on the USEPA Office of the Inspector General's *Scientific Analysis of Perchlorate (External Review Draft)*, dated December 30, 2008. Respondents include toxicologists and public health scientists at the Massachusetts Department of Environmental Protection (MassDEP), who participated in the development of the first state drinking water standard for perchlorate.

Overall comments relating to the draft report's preparation, release and conclusions are presented first, followed by a more specific discussion highlighting some of the technical limitations and uncertainties in the assessment. We believe these issues seriously undermine the draft report's analysis and conclusions.

Overall Comments. Although several of the technical aspects of the OIG assessment have merit, the overall document is, in several aspects, seriously flawed. In addition we are troubled by elements of the process followed in the preparation and release of this draft report.

Comment 1: The use of ICF Incorporated (Inc.) to provide technical review of this document prior to its release is troubling. ICF Inc. has provided considerable consulting services on perchlorate to at least one organization, the National Aeronautics and Space Administration, potentially subject to any USEPA regulatory determinations regarding this drinking water contaminant. This raises the appearance of a potential conflict of interest. In light of allegations of regulated industries' influence on certain USEPA policy and regulatory deliberations and decisions (e.g. as reported with respect to the Clean Air Mercury Rule), and in order to maximize process transparency, the USEPA should make the draft documents submitted to ICF Inc., as well as all comments and input provided by ICF Inc., available to the public.

Specific OIG Response:

MassDEP alleges a potential conflict of interest for the OIG because it hired a "defense industry contractor," ICF International, to perform a technical review on the *OIG Scientific Analysis of Perchlorate*. Before the release of the *OIG Scientific Analysis of Perchlorate*, the OIG decided to have an external party technically review our analysis before going public with it. Under the GSA e-buy Request for Quote (RFQ261223), on February 8, 2008, the OIG received only two bids, of which ICF International was determined to be the best qualified to conduct the technical review. Therefore, on March 3, 2008, the OIG contracted through the GSA with ICF Incorporated, LLC (ICF) under contract number GS-10F-0124J to conduct a 6-week technical review of a working draft of the *OIG Scientific Analysis of Perchlorate*. ICF International technical review supported the implementation of a cumulative risk assessment, but recommended using the "whole mixture" cumulative risk assessment approach using CDC's epidemiological analysis as opposed to our dose-addition method approach to the cumulative risk assessment.

In response to MassDEP's request for transparency of the process, the OIG is documenting the scientific comments made by ICF International on the *OIG Scientific Analysis of Perchlorate (Working Draft)* by providing the following two documents in Appendix D for the record:

- ICF International's Technical Review (Dated May 9, 2008) of the OIG Scientific Analysis of Perchlorate (Working Draft)

- OIG Workpaper documenting ICF International's May 21, 2008, presentation to the OIG on its Technical Review

Comment 2: It also appears that this document was rushed "out the door", as appropriate editing and review were clearly not completed. The report is often inconsistent and self contradictory; contains numerous distracting grammatical errors and several technical misstatements; and is incomplete with respect to discussion of scientific uncertainties. For example:
- The document incorrectly states that a reference dose (RfD) is "derived from a dose associated with an adverse effect" (pg. 43). In fact many RfD values are derived from "no adverse effect level" doses.
- The document also states that the USEPA perchlorate RfD was derived from a biological response (iodide uptake inhibition (IUI)) "several steps before the adverse effect (hypothyroidism) (pg. 45) but then subsequently demonstrates, compellingly, that adverse neurodevelopment outcomes in children are in fact associated with thyroid effects well prior to overt hypothyroidism. Indeed the OIG document makes a strong case that IUI is penultimate, rather than several steps upstream, to effects directly associated with adverse neurodevelopmental outcomes.
- Grammatical and typographical errors exist throughout the report.

Specific OIG Response:

In Section 5 of our report, we identify that EPA's risk assessment guidance defines an RfD as being derived from an adverse effect. Both a LOAEL and NOAEL are doses associated with an adverse effect (i.e., hence the "A" in the acronym). Therefore, an RfD is derived from a LOAEL or NOAEL to establish an exposure level that avoids the occurrence of this adverse effect from occurring in the public. By contrast, a NOEL is a dose that is associated with a biological event that is not an adverse effect. EPA risk assessment guidance does not support deriving an RfD from a NOEL. Furthermore, an RfD derived from an NOEL establishes an exposure level that avoids the occurrence of this biological event in the public. Shifting the EPA environmental risk management goal of avoiding adverse effects in humans to preventing the occurrence of an upstream biological effect is a significant change in environmental policy that represents a stricter criterion for protecting public health. Protecting against all biological effects is a momentous change in the EPA's environmental standard for protecting public health that would require a formal change in environmental policy, public law, environmental regulation, or EPA risk assessment guidance.

Both the NAS Committee and our report identify that the uptake of iodide is an upstream biological event that occurs before the onset of adverse effects at all life stages. The commenter mischaracterizes the uptake of iodide as being "penultimate" to adverse neurodevelopmental outcomes in children. Our analysis identifies that the NIS stress level acting on a pregnant mother in the range of 24.5% and 49% TIU is not sufficient to induce abnormal thyroid hormone levels. However, since the mother is providing the fetal environment, our report identifies that this same NIS stress level range acting on the fetal thyroid is sufficient to induce detectable adverse effects in the child. Our report identifies low fetal TIU as the precursor to the onset of first adverse effects.

MassDEP's comments appear to be based upon a fundamental difference in opinion rather than inconsistencies, contradictions, typographical errors, or grammatical errors. Whether the commenter regularly develops an RfD from a NOEL does not excuse the fact that the practice is contrary to EPA risk assessment guidance. The commenter's statement that the report supports the notion that iodide uptake inhibition (IUI) is penultimate is based upon the commenter's own mischaracterization of the report. OIG reports go through editing before release; however, that does not guarantee that all errors were identified and corrected. We are satisfied that the typos and grammatical errors were trivial. Further, identified errors have been addressed.

Comment 3: While cumulative effects on the thyroid gland are a valid issue to address, applying a new cumulative assessment methodology for determining an appropriate drinking water standard for perchlorate significantly deviates from longstanding USEPA protocols. Other drinking water standards and guidelines do not consider cumulative impacts nor has USEPA established a specific protocol for doing so. Is perchlorate an exception to the rule for standard setting or will the OIG recommend that USEPA consider cumulative effects for all other drinking water standards and health advisories? As a result of application of the cumulative effect approach, OIG appears to discount the need for a low perchlorate standard. Instead, OIG considers reassessing the nitrate drinking water standard, but favors adding iodine to prenatal vitamin supplements as the better alternative. However, protocols for these types of exposure standard tradeoffs and risk mitigation measures through dietary treatments do not exist, have never been vetted publically and have not been used with other chemicals. For example, calcium and iron have a protective effect with respect to lead exposures. Will OIG argue for a higher drinking water standard for lead with dietary supplementation with calcium and iron as an alternative? Due to these issues we believe such new protocols should be developed through a public process prior to their application on a chemical with such nationwide significance to public health. We recommend that USEPA's protocol for assessing mixtures to evaluate risks of multiple chemicals acting via the same mechanism of action be used to address perchlorate within a mixture of thyroid toxicants in water supplies, which would support a lower, more protective standard for perchlorate as discussed in comment 4.

Specific OIG Response:

The commenter advocates that EPA continue to use the single chemical risk assessment method, but apparently ignores that this method is ill suited to assess the risk from multiple concurrent exposures acting through the same mechanism of toxicity. Our report shows that the cumulative risk assessment approach is predictive and independently verifiable, whereas the single chemical method is not. We do not support advocating for an old risk assessment process that uses UFs to account for the lack of scientific knowledge. This report focused on implementing a cumulative risk assessment and other NAS recommendations to reduce the uncertainty in characterizing the public risk to exposure to NIS stress. Our report does not attempt to predict how cumulative risk assessments will be implemented by the Agency on other environmental exposures. However, our report does show that the cumulative risk assessment is viable now, not decades from now.

The comment makes several mischaracterizations. Our cumulative risk assessment acts on recommendations made over the last two decades to improve the characterization of risk. Our report challenges EPA's longstanding utilization of the outdated single chemical risk assessment approach that was initially developed to characterize risk by Dr. Lehman and Dr. Fitzhugh of the FDA in 1954. The current EPA risk assessment guidance directs risk assessors to consider and implement, if appropriate, a cumulative risk assessment when the chemicals share the same mechanism of toxicity and induce the same adverse effect(s), and when the relative potencies and the interaction between the chemicals are known.

Our cumulative risk assessment evaluated the incremental risk that exposure to each of the NIS stressors contributes to the occurrence of adverse effects in humans. Our analysis identified that further limiting the public's exposure to perchlorate below the RfD of 0.0007 mg/kg-day has only a minimal effect on lowering the occurrence of adverse effects in humans. In other words, even if perchlorate exposure could be eliminated in the U.S. population, this amount of NIS stress reduction is ineffective at significantly lowering the occurrence of adverse effects in children born to mothers exposed to excessive NIS stress from iodide deficiency during pregnancy and lactation. Our recommendation to consider iodide supplementation during pregnancy and lactation does not represent a "tradeoff in risk mitigation measures," but is the only viable remedy that significantly lowers the occurrence of neurodevelopmental effects occurring in children born to mothers with an elevated NIS stress level from iodide deficiency during pregnancy and lactation.

Comment 4: Although OIG's use of a cumulative effect approach may have merit, it is inappropriately used to argue against a protective drinking water value for perchlorate. In our view, from a public health perspective and a desire to protect children's health, exposures to multiple thyroid toxicants should lower the acceptable exposure value for any single toxicant not the other way around. OIG's conclusion that reliance on iodide supplementation through vitamins is an adequate public health response to contaminated drinking water supplies inappropriately shifts the responsibility for protecting public health from the polluter to the individual. It also affords those most at risk, the fetus and neonate, with no ability to protect their own health. Under this intervention approach, protection of infants from adverse health effects attributable to contaminated water supplies is completely dependent on the mother's ability to obtain necessary iodide supplementation and then to follow the recommended supplementation regimen, which may not always be possible due to individual circumstances and variability in the actual iodide content of vitamins, as has recently been reported (Boston Globe, 03/02/09)

Specific OIG Response:

Our analysis does not argue "against a protective drinking water value," but was done to better characterize the public health risk so that a protective exposure level could be identified with a higher level of confidence. Our analysis uses a different risk assessment technique and independently confirms that the NAS Committee's recommended perchlorate RfD of 0.0007 mg/kg-day is conservative and protective of human health.

The conventional wisdom might suggest that exposure to multiple toxicants acting through the same mechanism of toxicity should lower the acceptable exposure to each individual toxicant. This is probably the case when the multiple toxicants have the same potencies, the exposure levels to each toxicant are similar, and the exposure levels are sufficiently close to the acceptable exposure level. However, as seen in our cumulative risk assessment, characterizing the risk from multiple toxicant exposures is complex and the resulting findings depend on the particular factors involved.

We disagree with the characterization that our recommendation to consider iodide supplementation during pregnancy and lactation "inappropriately shifts" the responsibility from the polluter to the individual. This characterization of the public health issue clearly demonstrates that MassDEP does not appreciate the incremental risk that exposure to each of the individual NIS stressors contributes to this public health issue. Our analysis demonstrates that even if perchlorate exposure could be eliminated in the U.S. population, this amount of NIS stress reduction is ineffective at significantly lowering the occurrence of adverse effects in children born to mothers exposed to excessive NIS stress from iodide deficiency during pregnancy and lactation. Our recommendation does not shift responsibility, but is the only viable remedy that significantly lowers the occurrence of neurodevelopmental effects occurring in children born to mothers with an elevated NIS stress level from iodide deficiency during pregnancy and lactation.

Comment 5: OIG's conclusion that "the most effective and efficient approach for reducing health risks of permanent mental deficits in children from low maternal thyroid iodide uptake during pregnancy and nursing is to add iodide to all prenatal vitamins". One water supply in MA had perchlorate at a concentration of 1300 ppb. At this level, iodide supplementation is not likely to protect public health.

Specific OIG Response:

NAS proposed an RfD that EPA translated into a drinking water equivalent level (DWEL) of 24.5 ppb not 1300 ppb (53 times higher). Therefore, the comment mischaracterizes our report. Our report independently confirms, by using a completely different risk assessment technique, that the NAS Committee's recommended perchlorate RfD of 0.0007 mg/kg-day is conservative and protective of public health. Our report **does not** propose raising the perchlorate DWEL in drinking water above 24.5 ppb. Our report evaluates the amount of potential risk reduction to public health if the maximum allowable perchlorate concentration in drinking water is lowered from 24.5 ppb to 6.1 ppb. In our opinion, a drinking water supply with a perchlorate concentration of 1300 ppb poses an unacceptable risk to public health.

Additional Technical Comments.

Comment 6: The OIG assessment relies upon the Clewell *et al.* physiologically based pharmacokinetic (PBPK) model to predict iodide uptake. The uncertainties and limitations of this model were not considered despite the fact that questions have been raised regarding aspects of the model, in particular its applicability to the fetus and neonate, the groups of most concern.

Specific OIG Response:

Our analysis identified that in 1994, NAS recommended in *Science and Judgment in Risk Assessment* that EPA to use PBPK models to *reduce the uncertainty* by improving the measurement of exposure by identifying and using a chemical dose actually reaching the target tissue. An external dose is a poor measure of exposure. The actual internal exposure from the same external dose can easily vary up to a factor of five across life stages. This is observed with perchlorate and is document in Clewell PBPK Model (Clewell 2007, table 4). The use of the Clewell PBPK Model to estimate internal perchlorate exposure actually reduces the uncertainty in the risk assessment.

The Clewell PBPK Model has been under development for years and has undergone several revisions to improve its performance. The Clewell PBPK Model has been successfully corroborated against observed perchlorate blood serum concentrations in pregnant women, fetuses, and children, and against observed perchlorate concentration in breast milk. (Clewell 2007, figures 10 and 11). Although no model perfectly mimics reality, the Clewell PBPK Model has been sufficiently corroborated to allow its use in environmental risk assessments.

This comment captures a specific example of the risk assessment community's failure to accept corroborated innovative methods in the risk assessment process. In 1994, a NAS Committee recommended the use of PBPK models to reduce the uncertainty in environmental risk assessments. However, after 16 years, the risk assessment community is still arguing over the use of PBPK models in environmental risk assessment. Our report highlights the need for EPA to break away from the status quo single chemical risk assessment approach and implement the numerous risk assessment recommendations made over the last 20 years to make a significant breakthrough and improve the environmental risk assessment process.

Comment 7: The OIG assessment assumes a constant proportionality between thyroidal iodide uptake and concentrations in the serum/urine as advanced by Tonacchera *et al.* (2004). Although this assumption may be appropriate for the *in vitro*, petri dish experiments performed by Tonacchera *et al.*, this is an oversimplification that ignores adaptive responses which occur *in vivo*, as well as uncertainties regarding the cumulative impacts of exposures to sodium iodide symporter (NIS) inhibitors on the thyroid and other tissues expressing this protein. Specifically, the OIG document used the *in vitro* study of Tonacchera *et al.* (2004) to estimate the interaction and total amount of iodide uptake inhibition in the thyroid caused by perchlorate, thiocyanate, and nitrate. This analysis was described as a dose addition method. However, the simple kinetic equations used in the document (pg. 39, 72, 132, etc.) which were derived from the Tonacchera *et al. in vitro* lab study on Chinese hamster ovary cells expressing human NIS, do not adequately represent the *in vivo* workings of the hypothalamic-pituitary-thyroid axis. This approach does not account for the complex regulatory mechanisms involved in the modulation of iodide absorption, thyroid uptake, use and disposition. None-the-less, OIG based their analysis and conclusions on this *in vitro* approach with little discussion of the model's limitations and uncertainties. Reliance on such a simplistic approach to predict responses of such a complex system is fraught with uncertainty. Furthermore, even assuming that the Tonacchera model is accurate in predicting serum perchlorate equivalent concentrations (SPECs) in adults, the risk numbers derived by OIG based on the various studies and the derived SPECs are not themselves protective of the most sensitive subgroup, the neonate and the fetus.

The limitations of simple modeling approaches are further evidenced by the National Research Council (NRC) Perchlorate Committee (2005) use of Michaelis-Menton competitive inhibition equations to estimate the iodide uptake inhibition induced by perchlorate at various concentrations of perchlorate and iodide. They concluded that humans who have serum iodide concentrations of 0-1000 ug/L would be equally sensitive to perchlorate's effects on thyroid iodide uptake. However, studies conducted by Blount *et al.* (2006) and Stienmous *et al.* (2007) are inconsistent with this conclusion, as their results indicate that people with urine iodide levels less than 100 ug/L (assuming urine levels represent serum levels at steady state) are more sensitive to perchlorate's effect than people who have urine levels of iodine greater that 100 ug/L.

Specific OIG Response:

In our General Overall Response, we provided a detailed response to the issue of using *in vitro* data in an environmental risk assessment. We refer the commenter to this section as our response.

In regard to the CDC epidemiological analysis of the NHANES data, we have already provided an extensive response on this topic in Appendix A, response to ORD's and CDC's comments. We refer the commenter to these sections as our response.

Comment 8: OIG also downplayed important results by Steinmaus (2007). This well designed human study, which was conducted in the US, received only cursory review in Appendix A of the document while other human studies conducted in Chile and elsewhere were extensively reviewed in the body of the document. Stienmaus *et al.* concluded that thiocyanate and perchlorate, at a relatively low level, interact in affecting thyroid function in women with low urinary iodine. Thiocyanate alone at urine concentrations about 2000 times that of perchlorate was not associated with altered thyroid hormone levels in women with low urinary iodine levels, but significantly altered hormone levels were observed when perchlorate exposures were also considered. This interactive effect was observed at perchlorate and thiocyanate exposure levels documented to be occurring in the US.

Specific OIG Response:

The commenter praises the Steinmaus model but ignores that it cannot be verified and is contrary to accepted results. We conclude that the findings from the Steinmaus statistical model have not been corroborated by a different study design and population and therefore cannot be used for an environmental risk assessment. In short, the Steinmaus statistical model of the NHANES data identifies that thiocyanate has no independent effect on serum fT_4 but, rather acts as a "potentiator" of perchlorate's toxicity. However, this does not agree with the known toxicity of thiocyanate. Excessive exposure to thiocyanate in areas of endemic cretinism clearly shows that thiocyanate in conjunction with low iodide can induce low serum fT_4 values without the need for perchlorate exposure to induce toxicity. Furthermore, excessive exposure to thiocyanate is known to induce hypothyroxinemia in both men and women (Banerjee 1997; Banerjee 1997b) without the need for perchlorate exposure to induce toxicity. The assertion that thiocyanate acts as a 'potentiator' is not supported by any other dataset or analysis.

Comment 9: The OIG document also relied on the Tonacchera *et al.* model (pg 133) to justify the NRC (2005) statement that "To cause declines in thyroid hormone production that would have adverse health effects iodide uptake must likely be reduced by at least 75% for months or longer". In the OIG assessment the thyroid iodide uptake (TIU) that is associated with hypothyroidism ($TIU_{hypothyroidism}$) is calculated as the ratio of the urinary iodide concentration (UIC) associated with severe iodine deficiency (20 ug/L urine iodide) to the median UIC in healthy adults (150 ug/L urine iodide). On this basis OIG argues that the $TIU_{hypothyroidism}$ = 20 ug/L/150 ug/L x 100% = 13.3% of the "normal" uptake, which is equated to an 86.7% inhibition of iodide uptake. However, this calculation is overly simplistic as thyroid function is a complex process involving the up and down regulation of iodide uptake. The amount of iodide excreted in the urine in iodine deficient diets is relatively less than that in iodine sufficient diets, indicating that urinary iodide levels in iodine deficient individuals are not representative of ingested iodine levels or iodide uptake as suggested by the OIG document. It is also important to note that, although NIS up-regulation increases iodide uptake in iodine deficient animals, it does not necessarily prevent hormone alterations (Schroder-Van Der Elst *et al.* 2005), especially in fetuses. Therefore, the ratio determined in the previous paragraph is not a good measure of iodide uptake inhibition or its potential to cause adverse neurodevelopment effects in children.

Specific OIG Response:

Unchallenged, this mischaracterization of the content of our report is misleading and potentially detrimental to the process of characterizing and addressing this public health issue. Our report identifies that a %TIU of 13.3% is the estimated NIS stress level at which hypothyroidism is observed in adults. Our report does not state that a %TIU of 13.3% is protective. In Section 9.4.2 of our report, we identify that a %TIU of 49% is the NOAEL during pregnancy and lactation. Our analysis found no reported adverse effects in children when pregnancy and lactation occur at an NIS stress level above 49%. We applied a 1.5 safety factor to the NOAEL and recommended that the NIS stress level remain above a %TIU of 74% during pregnancy and lactation to avoid the occurrence of adverse neurodevelopment effects in children.

Comment 10: Although the OIG's use of thyroid effect data attributable to other NIS inhibitors is with merit and could provide useful information regarding effect levels, the assessment appears biased. The OIG report provides little evaluation of the limitations of the various epidemiological studies addressing other NIS inhibitors, which compromise their ability to accurately detect and estimate effects. In addition the RfD derivation using data from nitrate exposed populations inappropriately considered the enlarged thyroid effects observed to be non-adverse. This outcome should be considered an adverse health effect, which would lower the associated RfD for perchlorate to a value well below that derived by NRC/EPA.

Specific OIG Response:

In our General Overall Response, we provide an extensive discussion and comparison of uncertainties between the single chemical risk assessment approach and the cumulative risk assessment approach to this public health issue.

We disagree with the characterization that the enlarged thyroid reported in the Tajtáková nitrate exposure study (Tajtáková 2006) should have been considered an adverse effect. Any detectable biological change does not make it an adverse effect. In our General Overall Response, we discuss the difference between deriving an RfD from an adverse effect or a nonadverse effect. In short, deriving an RfD from a nonadverse effect shifts the environmental risk management goal of preventing adverse effects in humans to preventing all biological effects from exposure. This shift is a significant change in environmental policy. Protecting against all biological effects in humans from exposure is a stricter criterion for protecting public health than the traditional criterion of limiting exposure to protect against adverse effects in humans. Further, protecting against all biological effects would represent a momentous change in the EPA's environmental standard for protecting public health that would require a formal change in environmental policy, public law, environmental regulation, and EPA risk assessment guidance.

Comment 11: The OIG interpretation of the data in Braverman *et al.* (2005) is also incomplete. OIG assumed that the increased urinary iodide observed during perchlorate exposure compared to pre-exposure levels was due to increased ingestion of iodide during exposure and adjusted the calculations accordingly. Braverman *et al.* noted that the urinary iodine excretion among employees during perchlorate exposure was approximately 55% higher than in the pre-exposed state and stated that they found it unlikely that this was attributable to a short-term dietary change. Rather the authors suggested that the thyroid may be concentrating less of the dietary iodide during perchlorate exposure. Schroder-Van Der Elst *et al.* (2005) have also reported an increase in serum levels of iodide in perchlorate exposed rats.

Specific OIG Response:

The Braverman occupational study reports that the UIC among employees during perchlorate exposure was approximately 55% higher than in the employees in the pre-exposed state. The authors speculate that a short-term dietary change is unlikely to account for this difference, but suggest that the thyroid may be concentrating less of the dietary iodide during perchlorate exposure.

The commenter does not identify that mean UIC among employees during perchlorate exposure was statistically the same as the UIC of the controls (i.e., 230 ± 163 vs 296 ± 183 ug I⁻/g creatinine (p = 0.25), respectively). A more plausible account of this observation is the employees' thyroids have adapted to a higher NIS stress environment (e.g., up-regulated the expression of the NIS gene), which make their thyroid more efficient in uptaking iodide from the blood. For these employees, the high NIS stress environment is the normal state for their thyroids and this is why their UIC levels during perchlorate exposure are not statistically different than the controls (i.e., p = 0.25). For these employees, the abnormal NIS stress condition occurs when they are not at work being exposed to perchlorate. Braverman reports that the employees in the pre-exposed state have a statistically lower mean UIC of 148 ± 83 ug I⁻/g creatinine (p = 0.02). With a lower NIS stress level during pre-exposure, their up-regulated thyroids are more efficient at removing iodide from the blood leaving less to be excreted.

Braverman's hypothesis is that the thyroid may be concentrating less of the dietary iodide during perchlorate exposure. However, Braverman's hypothesis fails to explain why the UIC levels between the pre-exposed and controls are significantly different. The dietary iodide intake and UIC levels should be the same between the pre-exposed and controls. Braverman even argues that dietary iodide intake levels are fairly constant. By contrast, our hypothesis is the thyroid is concentrating more dietary iodide from the blood during pre-exposure (i.e., periods of low NIS stress). Our hypothesis accounts for the lower employee UIC levels during pre-exposure with the dietary iodide intake levels remaining the same between the employees and the controls. Our hypothesis explains the available data better.

The NAS Committee states that rats are more sensitive to the effects of NIS stress (NAS 2005, pp 168–69). Therefore, the rat studies are not appropriate for determining the dose-response relationship in humans (NAS 2005, pp 168–69). Therefore, the commenter's reference to the observations in a perchlorate rat study is not particularly meaningful.

Conclusion. In conclusion, the OIG assessment contains several technical limitations and inadequately considers the many scientific uncertainties involved in predicting thyroid iodide uptake and inhibition and risks of adverse neurodevelopmental effects in children. Due to these deficiencies, as well as the issues previously noted in the first section of these comments, the OIG's conclusions are questionable. Given widespread contamination of drinking water supplies and food items with perchlorate and other thyroid toxicants, MassDEP continues to believe that perchlorate levels in drinking water should not exceed 2 parts per billion in order to protect the fetus and neonate.

Specific OIG Response:

We thoroughly considered your comments. We believe our cumulative risk assessment decreases the uncertainty in the risk characterization of this public health issue as compared to a single chemical risk assessment approach. Further, unlike the single chemical risk approach, the cumulative approach is verifiable. Our report identifies that a further lowering of the perchlorate levels in drinking water to 2 ppb is not an effective approach to addressing this public health issue.

Sincerely,

Tsedash Zewdie, PhD
Toxicologist

Carol Rowan-West, MSPH
Director Office of Research and Standards

C. Mark Smith PhD, SM
Deputy Director Office of Research and
Standards and Toxicologist

References citations provided with MassDEP's comments are not repeated here but are available in Appendix D.

OIG Response to Consultants in Epidemiology and Occupational Health, LLC's Comments

The submission from Consultants in Epidemiology and Occupational Health, LLC, provided us with additional scientific paper for consideration. Although we would like to further develop and refine our cumulative risk assessment approach, our primary mission is not to conduct environmental risk assessments. We conducted this cumulative risk assessment to demonstrate, by example, how the numerous recommendations on how to improve environmental risk assessments over the last two decades could actually be implemented. We refer the commenter to review our General Overall Response, which expresses our overall response to the fundamental scientific issues raised by the commenters.

The comments from Consultants in Epidemiology and Occupational Health, LLC, on our external review draft are provided in their entirety in Appendix D.

OIG Response to the Environmental Working Group's Comments

The submission from the EWG is a position paper that rationalizes EWG's agenda for stringent regulation of perchlorate exposure. We consider this unresponsive to our request for scientific and technical comments on our implementation of a cumulative risk assessment to characterize the risk from exposure to the NIS stressors. Therefore, a scientific response is not warranted. However, we refer the commenter to review our General Overall Response, which expresses our overall response to the fundamental scientific issues raised by the commenters.

The comments from the EWG on our external review draft are provided in their entirety in Appendix D.

OIG Response to Human Health Risk Research, Inc.'s Comments

The comments from Human Health Risk Research, Inc. support the use a cumulative risk assessment to characterize the risk of this public health issue. The majority of its comments provide additional information on the Greer human perchlorate exposure study. However, Human Health Risk Research, Inc. makes the following two points:

- The commenter identifies that the word "total" is not informative in the context of iodide uptake.

  OIG Response:

  Our intent in using the word "total" in our cumulative risk assessment was to express that the combined stress from the concurrent exposure to all four NIS stressors results in the final "total" amount of iodide uptake by the thyroid. In a typical perchlorate-only exposure study, exposure to the other three NIS stressors was neither controlled nor measured, leaving them to act as confounding factors. Therefore, considerable amount of uncertainty is introduced in the experimental design. The change in the observed iodide uptake between the exposed group and the control group may or may not be the sole result of the effect from perchlorate exposure, but may include the effect from a change in exposure to one or more the other NIS stress between the exposed group and the control group.

- The commenter identifies that a sustained exposure to a low iodide uptake is needed to induce adverse effect.

    OIG Response:

    We agree that a sustained exposure to a low iodide uptake is needed to induce an adverse effect. When we selected exposure studies for the identification of when an adverse effect occurs in adults, males or females, pregnant women, or fetuses, we only used studies where the elevated NIS stress level was sustained over a long period of time (e.g., months). However, the minimum duration of time needed to induce an adverse effect(s) is not exactly known.

We refer the commenter to review our General Overall Response, which expresses our overall response to the fundamental scientific issues raised by the commenters.

The comments from Human Health Risk Research on our external review draft are provided in their entirety in Appendix D.

OIG Response to Intertox, Inc.'s Comments

The submission from Intertox on behalf of the Perchlorate Study Group (PSG) is a position paper. However, Intertox does provide several scientific comments (e.g., protein binding) that could be used to further develop and refine a cumulative risk assessment approach to characterizing this public health issue. However, our primary mission is not to conduct environmental risk assessments. We conducted this cumulative risk assessment to demonstrate, by example, how the numerous recommendations on how to improve environmental risk assessments could actually be implemented. Furthermore, we conducted this cumulative risk assessment to independently evaluate if the NAS Committee's recommend RfD of 0.0007 mg/kg-day is protective of human health. Therefore, we refer the commenter to review our General Overall Response, which expresses our overall response to the fundamental scientific issues raised by the commenters.

The comments from Intertox, Inc., on our external review draft are provided in their entirety in Appendix D.

OIG Response to Opdebeeck Consulting, Sarl's Comments

The comments from Opdebeeck Consulting support the use a cumulative risk assessment to characterize the risk of this public health issue. Furthermore, its comments support the inclusion of the lack of iodide stressor in the cumulative risk assessment of this public health issue.

The majority of Opdebeeck Consulting's comments dealt with the derivation of a perchlorate RSC. However, our analysis conducted a cumulative risk assessment to evaluate the protectiveness of the perchlorate RfD. Our analysis did not specifically evaluate EPA's derivation of the perchlorate RSC. EPA's derivation of the proposed perchlorate RSC occurred after our field work and, therefore, was not included in our science review. Thus, we will not provide comments concerning the RSC. We refer the commenter to review our General Overall Response, which expresses our overall response to the fundamental scientific issues raised by the commenters.

The comments from Opdebeeck Consulting, Sarl on our external review draft are provided in their entirety in Appendix D.